24

STUDY GUIDE

Crime and Punishment in Britain, c1000-Present and Whitechapel, c1870-c1900: Crime, Policing and the Inner City

Edexcel - GCSE

app available

Published by Clever Lili Limited.

contact@cleverlili.com

First published 2020

ISBN 978-1-913887-23-0

Cover by: Tony Baggett on Adobe Stock

Icons by: flaticon and freepik

Contributors: Helen LambJen Mellors, Marcus Pailing, Shahan Abu Shumel Haydar, Jen Mellors

Edited by Paul Connolly and Rebecca Parsley

Design by Evgeni Veskov and Will Fox

DISCOVER MORE OF OUR GCSE HISTORY STUDY GUIDES

GCSEHistory.com and Clever Lili

Edexcel - GCSE

STUDY GUIDE

Short Sample

GCSEHistory.com

Edexcel - GCSE

STUDY GUIDE

Short Sample 2

GCSEHistory.com

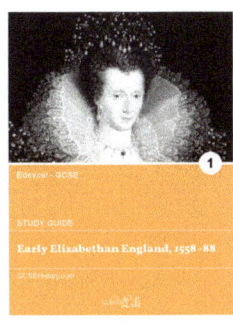

Edexcel - GCSE

STUDY GUIDE

Early Elizabethan England, 1558-88

GCSEHistory.com

Edexcel - GCSE

STUDY GUIDE

Medicine in Britain, c1250–Present and The British Sector of the Western Front, 1914-18: Injuries, Treatment and the Trenches

GCSEHistory.com

Edexcel - GCSE

STUDY GUIDE

Weimar and Nazi Germany, 1918-39

GCSEHistory.com

Edexcel - GCSE

STUDY GUIDE

Superpower Relations and the Cold War, 1941-91

GCSEHistory.com

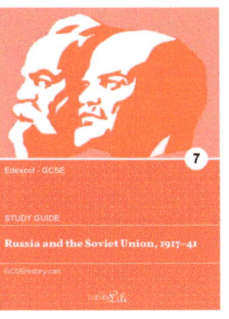

Edexcel - GCSE

STUDY GUIDE

Russia and the Soviet Union, 1917-41

GCSEHistory.com

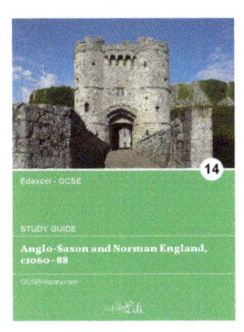

Edexcel - GCSE

STUDY GUIDE

Anglo-Saxon and Norman England, c1060-88

GCSEHistory.com

Edexcel - GCSE

STUDY GUIDE

The USA, 1954-75: Conflict at Home and Abroad

GCSEHistory.com

Edexcel - GCSE

STUDY GUIDE

The American West, c1835-c1895

GCSEHistory.com

THE GUIDES ARE EVEN BETTER WITH OUR GCSE/IGCSE HISTORY WEBSITE APP AND MOBILE APP

GCSE History is a text and voice web and mobile app that allows you to easily revise for your GCSE/IGCSE exams wherever you are - it's like having your own personal GCSE history tutor. Whether you're at home or on the bus, GCSE History provides you with thousands of convenient bite-sized facts to help you pass your exams with flying colours. We cover all topics - with more than 120,000 questions - across the Edexcel, AQA and CIE exam boards.

Contents

In this study guide, you will see a series of icons, highlighted words and page references. The key below will help you quickly establish what these mean and where to go for more information.

Icons

 WHAT questions cover the key events and themes.

 WHO questions cover the key people involved.

 WHEN questions cover the timings of key events.

 WHERE questions cover the locations of key moments.

 WHY questions cover the reasons behind key events.

 HOW questions take a closer look at the way in which events, situations and trends occur.

 IMPORTANCE questions take a closer look at the significance of events, situations, and recurrent trends and themes.

DECISIONS questions take a closer look at choices made at events and situations during this era.

Highlighted words

Abdicate - occasionally, you will see certain words highlighted within an answer. This means that, if you need it, you'll find an explanation of the word or phrase in the glossary which starts on **page 127**.

Page references

Tudor *(p. 7)* - occasionally, a certain subject within an answer is covered in more depth on a different page. If you'd like to learn more about it, you can go directly to the page indicated.

Crime and Punishment in Britain c1000 - Present is a thematic study that looks at the change and continuity of crime and punishment across a broad sweep of British history. You will look at the main people, events and developments, as well as significant features of the different ages, from medieval to modern times. In studying Whitechapel, you will investigate a historic environment that was significant to crime and punishment and the events and developments that occurred there.

Purpose

In studying this course you will understand the wider themes of societal change and control. You will investigate the conditions that shaped attitudes towards crime and punishment, be able to view the process of change and continuity across time, and make comparisons between different ages. Through the study of Whitechapel, you will develop an understanding of the use of sources in a historical enquiry.

Topics

Crime and Punishment in Britain c1000 - Present is split into five key topics:

- c1000-c1500 looks at change and continuity in crime, punishment and law enforcement from the Anglo-Saxons, through the Norman conquest, and during the late medieval period.

- c1500-c1700 examines the early modern era, from the Tudors to the Enlightenment, considering the impact of the Gunpowder Plot, the witch hunts and the English Civil War.

- c1700-c1900 looks at the industrial age and the way changes to society impacted on crime, punishment and law enforcement. This includes the development of the police, the changing nature of punishment and new definitions of crime.

- c1900-present follows the change and continuity in crime, punishment and law enforcement in the modern age.

- Whitechapel 1870-1900 examines the historic environment of Whitechapel, its conditions, people and society, as well as policing in the area and the response to the case of Jack the Ripper.

Case Studies

Through the course there are a number of case studies that allow you to investigate crime, punishment and law enforcement through the study of a single person, event or institution.

- The crime, punishment and the medieval church case study covers c1000-1500. This covers the influence of the church on crime and punishment, sanctuary, benefit of clergy and the use (and end) of trials by ordeal.

- For 1500-1700 and early modern crime and punishment, the case studies are the Gunpowder Plot of 1604 and the witch hunts of 1645-47.

- In the study of crime and punishment in industrial Britain, 1700-1900, the case studies are Pentonville Prison and the role of Robert Peel.

- In the study of modern crime and punishment 1900-present, the case studies are the Derek Bentley case of 1953, and conscientious objectors.

- Whitechapel 1870-1900 is the largest and most in-depth case study.

Key Individuals

Some of the key individuals studied on this course include:

- William I.
- Henry II and Thomas Becket.
- The Tudor monarchs.
- James I.
- Guy Fawkes and the Gunpowder Plotters.
- Matthew Hopkins.
- John Howard and Elizabeth Fry.
- Robert Peel.
- Jack the Ripper.
- Timothy Evans.
- Derek Bentley.
- Ruth Ellis.

Key Themes

Some of the key themes you will study on this course include:

- The changing definitions of crime.
- The nature of crimes committed during a particular period or age.
- Law enforcement, including preventing and detecting crime, and catching the criminal.
- The process of determining guilt and criminal trials.
- The changing nature and purpose of punishments.
- The social conditions that influenced these changes.

Assessment

Crime and Punishment in Britain c1000 - Present is assessed by Paper 1 and is worth 30% of your overall grade. The paper is split into two sections.

- Section A focuses on the historical environment of Whitechapel. This consists of a knowledge-based question and a two-part question based on two historical sources.
- Section B contains three questions that assess your knowledge and understanding of the thematic part of the course.

Section A

Section A contains Question 1, a knowledge-based question, and Question 2, a two-part question based on two sources.

- Question 1 is worth 4 marks. It will ask you describe two features of the historical environment of Whitechapel.
- Question 2(a) is worth 8 marks. It will ask you about the usefulness of two sources in reference to a particular historical enquiry. You will be required to refer to both sources and your own knowledge in your answer.
- Question 2(b) is worth 4 marks. It will ask how you would follow up on one of the sources to continue the particular historical enquiry. You will be required to choose a detail from the source to continue your study, to give a question you could ask to find out more, the type of source that you could use for your investigation and to explain how that would help your enquiry.

Section B

Section B contains Question 3, an explanation of similarities between different periods and Question 4, an explanation of change or consequence. You will have a choice of one between Questions 5 and 6, which will give you a historical interpretation to support and challenge.

- Question 3 is worth 4 marks. It will ask you to compare an issue across two different periods of time.

Revision! A dreaded word. Everyone knows it's coming, everyone knows how much it helps with your exam performance, and everyone struggles to get started! We know you want to do the best you can in your GCSEs, but schools aren't always clear on the best way to revise. This can leave students wondering:

- ✔ How should I plan my revision time?
- ✔ How can I beat procrastination?
- ✔ What methods should I use? Flash cards? Re-reading my notes? Highlighting?

Luckily, you no longer need to guess at the answers. Education researchers have looked at all the available revision studies, and the jury is in. They've come up with some key pointers on the best ways to revise, as well as some thoughts on popular revision methods that aren't so helpful. The next few pages will help you understand what we know about the best revision methods.

How can I beat procrastination?

This is an age-old question, and it applies to adults as well! Have a look at our top three tips below.

⊚ Reward yourself

When we think a task we have to do is going to be boring, hard or uncomfortable, we often put if off and do something more 'fun' instead. But we often don't really enjoy the 'fun' activity because we feel guilty about avoiding what we should be doing. Instead, get your work done and promise yourself a reward after you complete it. Whatever treat you choose will seem all the sweeter, and you'll feel proud for doing something you found difficult. Just do it!

⊚ Just do it!

We tend to procrastinate when we think the task we have to do is going to be difficult or dull. The funny thing is, the most uncomfortable part is usually making ourselves sit down and start it in the first place. Once you begin, it's usually not nearly as bad as you anticipated.

⊚ Pomodoro technique

The pomodoro technique helps you trick your brain by telling it you only have to focus for a short time. Set a timer for 20 minutes and focus that whole period on your revision. Turn off your phone, clear your desk, and work. At the end of the 20 minutes, you get to take a break for five. Then, do another 20 minutes. You'll usually find your rhythm and it becomes easier to carry on because it's only for a short, defined chunk of time.

Spaced practice

We tend to arrange our revision into big blocks. For example, you might tell yourself: "This week I'll do all my revision for the Cold War, then next week I'll do the Medicine Through Time unit."

This is called **massed practice**, because all revision for a single topic is done as one big mass.

But there's a better way! Try **spaced practice** instead. Instead of putting all revision sessions for one topic into a single block, space them out. See the example below for how it works.

This means planning ahead, rather than leaving revision to the last minute - but the evidence strongly suggests it's worth it. You'll remember much more from your revision if you use **spaced practice** rather than organising it into big blocks. Whichever method you choose, though, remember to reward yourself with breaks.

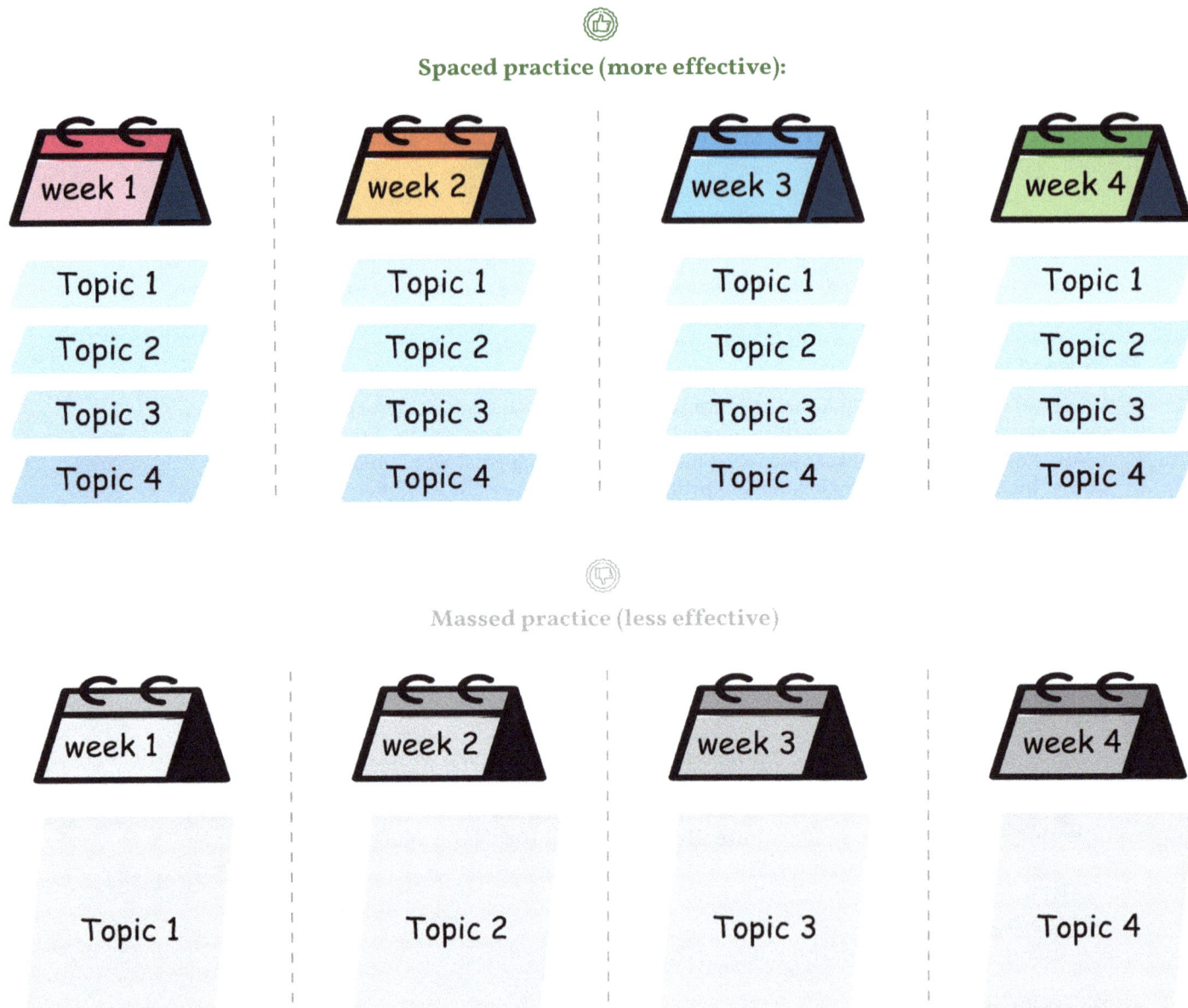

What methods should I use to revise?

Self-testing/flash cards	Self explanation/mind-mapping

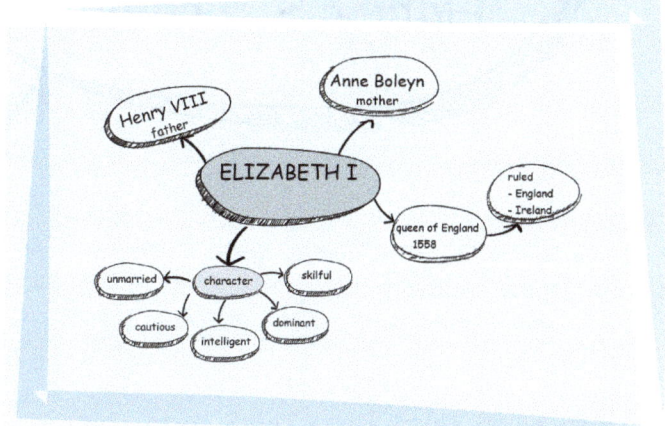

The research shows a clear winner for revision methods - **self-testing**. A good way to do this is with **flash cards.** Flash cards are really useful for helping you recall short – but important – pieces of information, like names and dates.

Side A - question	Side B - answer

Write questions on one side of the cards, and the answers on the back. This makes answering the questions and then testing yourself easy. Put all the cards you get right in a pile to one side, and only repeat the test with the ones you got wrong - this will force you to work on your weaker areas.

pile with right answers	pile with wrong answers

As this book has a quiz question structure itself, you can use it for this technique.

Another good revision method is **self-explanation**. This is where you explain how and why one piece of information from your course linked with another piece.

This can be done with **mind-maps**, where you draw the links and then write explanations for how they connect. For example, President Truman is connected with anti-communism because of the Truman Doctrine.

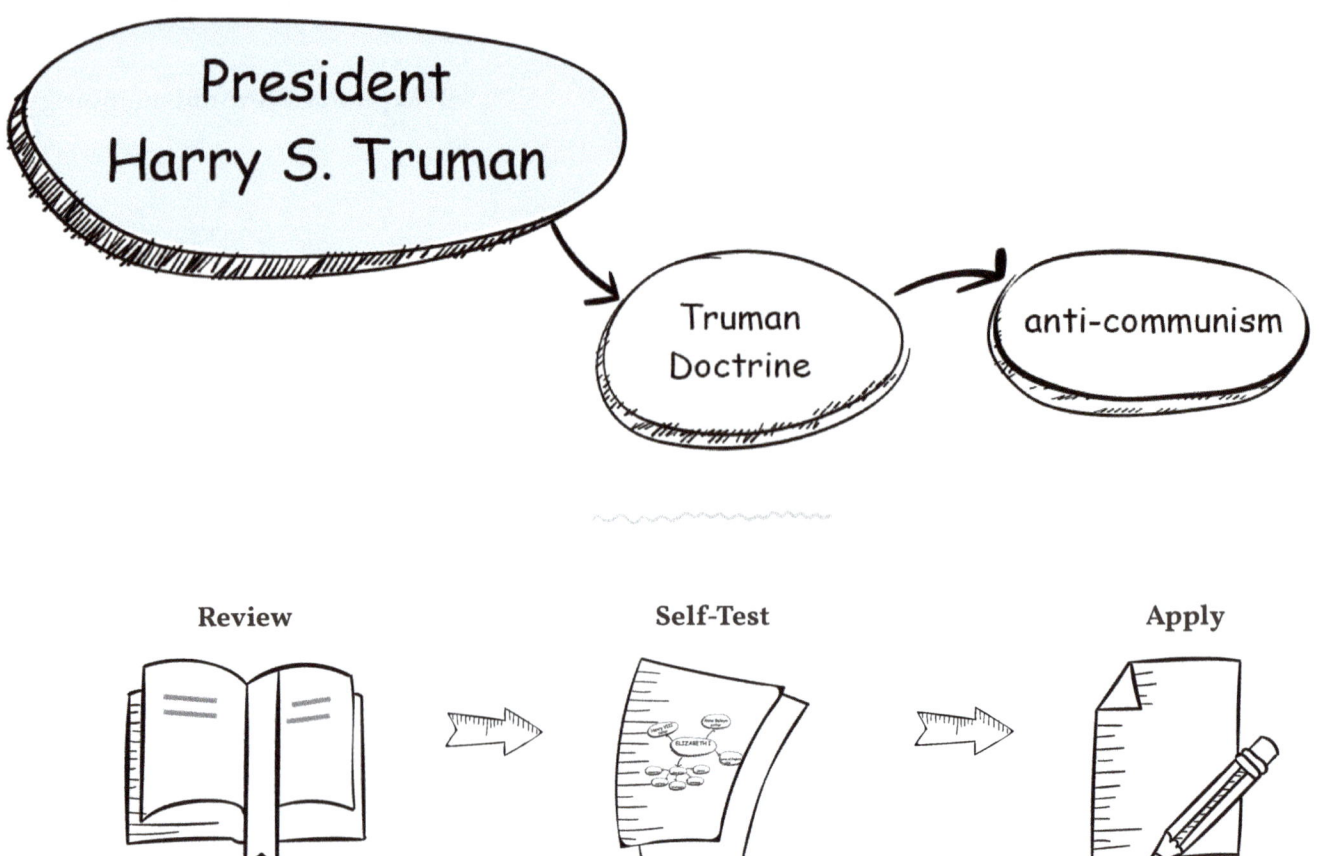

Review	Self-Test	Apply
Start by highlighting or re-reading to create your flashcards for self-testing.	Test yourself with flash cards. Make mind maps to explain the concepts.	Apply your knowledge on practice exam questions.

 ### Which revision techniques should I be cautious about?

Highlighting and **re-reading** are not necessarily bad strategies - but the research does say they're less effective than flash cards and mind-maps.

If you do use these methods, make sure they are **the first step to creating flash cards**. Really engage with the material as you go, rather than switching to autopilot.

Quizzes, amazing exam preparation tools and more at GCSEHistory.com

TIMELINE

Murdrum laws introduced *(p.26)*

1070

1072 The Forest Laws made it illegal to hunt without a licence on the king's land *(p.26)* .

Parliament defined vagrancy and treason *(p.29)* **1351**

1494 The Beggars and Vagabonds Act introduced *(p.47)*

The Witchcraft Act made witchcraft a capital crime *(p.39)* **1542**

1559 The Act of Uniformity made it illegal to miss church *(p.33)*

Adultery became punishable by death *(p.43)* **1650**

1736 The Witchcraft Act redefined witchcraft as a form of fraud *(p.39)*

Under the Bloody Code, there were 225 capital crimes *(p.63)* **1815**

1916 The Military Conscription Act *(p.108)*

The Race Relations Act *(p.87)* **1965**

1967 Homosexuality legalised in the Sexual Offences Act *(p.85)*

The Misuse of Drugs Act *(p.89)* **1971**

2005 The Criminal Justice Act *(p.86)*

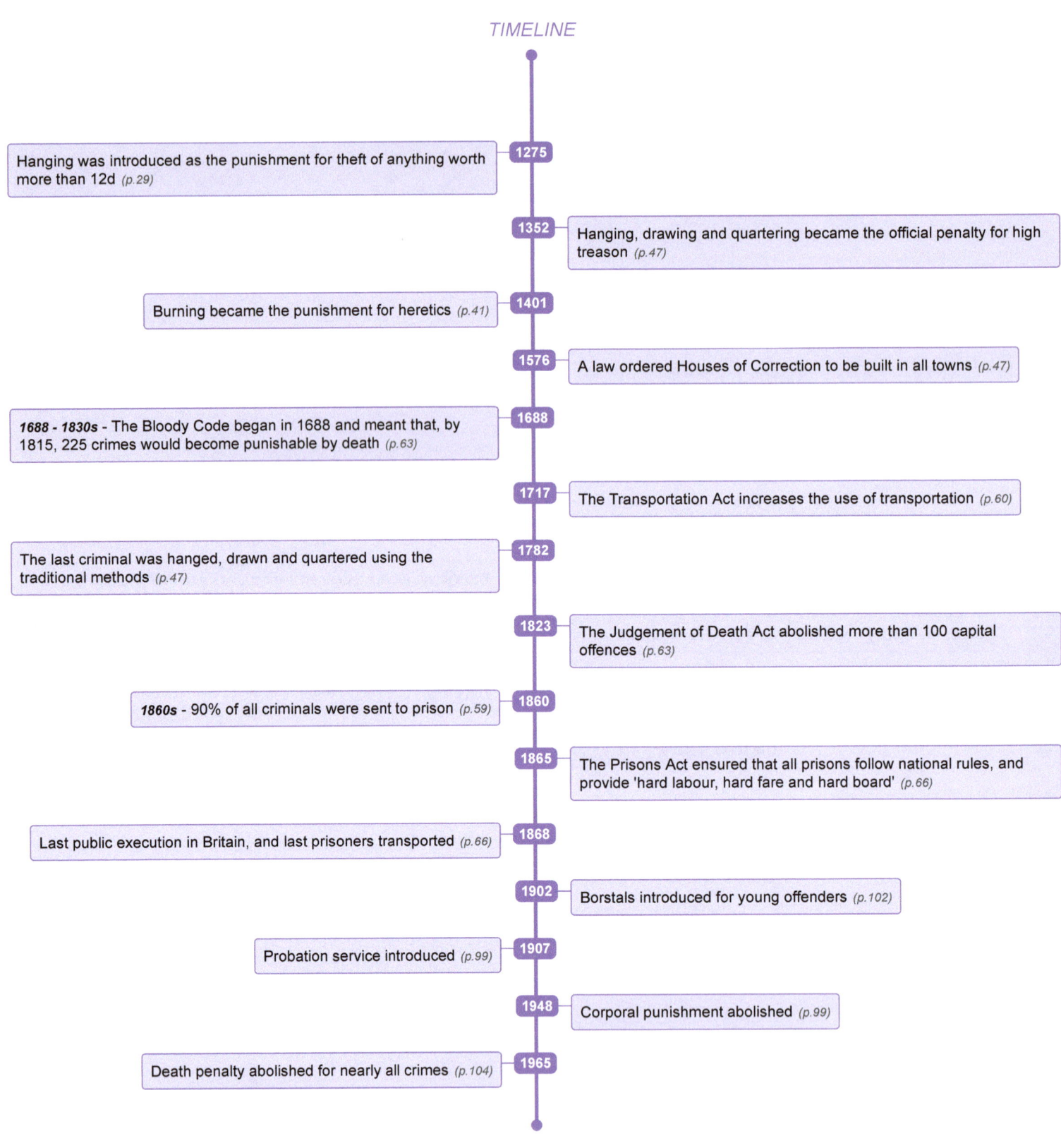

TIMELINE

1275 — Hanging was introduced as the punishment for theft of anything worth more than 12d *(p.29)*

1352 — Hanging, drawing and quartering became the official penalty for high treason *(p.47)*

1401 — Burning became the punishment for heretics *(p.41)*

1576 — A law ordered Houses of Correction to be built in all towns *(p.47)*

1688 — *1688 - 1830s* - The Bloody Code began in 1688 and meant that, by 1815, 225 crimes would become punishable by death *(p.63)*

1717 — The Transportation Act increases the use of transportation *(p.60)*

1782 — The last criminal was hanged, drawn and quartered using the traditional methods *(p.47)*

1823 — The Judgement of Death Act abolished more than 100 capital offences *(p.63)*

1860 — *1860s* - 90% of all criminals were sent to prison *(p.59)*

1865 — The Prisons Act ensured that all prisons follow national rules, and provide 'hard labour, hard fare and hard board' *(p.66)*

1868 — Last public execution in Britain, and last prisoners transported *(p.66)*

1902 — Borstals introduced for young offenders *(p.102)*

1907 — Probation service introduced *(p.99)*

1948 — Corporal punishment abolished *(p.99)*

1965 — Death penalty abolished for nearly all crimes *(p.104)*

TIMELINE

Archbishop Lanfranc separated Church courts from law courts *(p.31)* — **1076**

1170 — The murder of Thomas Becket prevented Henry II from controlling Church courts *(p.31)*

1194-1195 - Coroners and 'Keepers of the King's Peace' introduced *(p.29)* — **1194**

1215 — Trials by ordeal ended *(p.23)*

Keepers of the King's Peace became Justices of the Peace *(p.37)* — **1361**

1603 — The JPs enforced over 300 laws *(p.45)*

1690s - 'Revenue Men of the Customs and Excise' introduced to tackle smuggling *(p.58)* — **1690**

1725 — Jonathan Wild, the 'Thief-Taker General', hanged for his crimes *(p.46)*

Bow Street Runners set up by Henry Fielding *(p.73)* — **1748**

1829 — Robert Peel's Metropolitan Police Act *(p.74)*

A regular detective branch, with 16 officers, was set up at Scotland Yard *(p.74)* — **1842**

1856 — The Police Act forced all counties to set up a police force *(p.77)*

Special Branch established *(p.74)* — **1883**

1971 — The Courts Act *(p.81)*

Neighbourhood Watch set up *(p.97)* — **1982**

TIMELINE

The Norman Conquest *(p.26)* — **1066**

1348 — *1348-1351* - The Black Death *(p.29)*

The Peasants' Revolt *(p.29)* — **1381**

1455 — *1455-1485* - The War of the Roses *(p.29)*

The printing press was brought to London *(p.34)* — **1476**

1530 — *1530s* - Break with Rome and start of the English Reformation *(p.34)*

1642-1660 - The English Civil Wars and Protectorate — **1642**

1680 — *1680 - 1830* - The Enlightenment *(p.52)*

1750-1900 - The Industrial Revolution *(p.52)* — **1750**

1830 — *1830 - 1850* - Railways built to connect most of the major towns in Britain *(p.52)*

Middle-class men received the vote *(p.52)* — **1832**

1870 — The Education Act - school for all children up to 10 *(p.52)*

1914-1918 - First World War *(p.81)* — **1914**

1928 — All British men and women over 21 can vote *(p.81)*

1939-1945 - Second World War *(p.81)* — **1939**

1995 — The internet was put to common use *(p.81)*

CRIME AND PUNISHMENT - EVENTS IN BRITAIN

DEFINITIONS OF CRIME

'Every society has the criminals that it deserves.' - Havelock Ellis

What is crime?

A crime is an act considered unlawful and punishable by a government or other authority.

How is crime divided?

Criminal activity is divided into 3 different types.

- ☑ Crimes against the person, such as murder, assault and rape.
- ☑ Crimes against property, such as theft, robbery and smuggling *(p.58)*.
- ☑ Crimes against authority, such as heresy *(p.41)*, treason and illegal protest.

What is the definition of social crime?

A social crime is an act most people don't believe is criminal and which they are prepared to commit or ignore.

What is the definition of moral crime?

Moral crimes are actions that don't physically harm anyone or their property, but which don't match society's views of decent behaviour. Examples include having sex outside marriage or not following Church rules.

What sort of crime is a felony?

A felony is a crime considered very serious by society.

What is a petty crime?

'Petty' is the name given to crimes that are seen as minor or less serious.

What is the crime of petty theft?

Petty theft is the stealing of small, low-value items.

What is the crime of treason?

Treason is an action against the government or other rulers.

What is the crime of heresy?

Heresy *(p.41)* is the crime of going against the teachings of the Church. This was strongly enforced at certain times throughout history.

What is the crime of arson?

Arson is to deliberately set fire to a public or private building or property.

What is a crime of public disorder?

Public disorder offences occur when someone's behaviour in public causes - or may cause - distress or harassment to anyone present.

DEFINITIONS OF PUNISHMENT

'I am told that the proximity of punishment arouses real repentance in the criminal...' - Dostoyevsky

What are punishments?

Punishments are the actions taken in response to crime by the authorities or ruling group in any society.

What are the different sorts of punishment?

There are 5 main methods a society might decide to use to punish its members for crime:

- ☑ Capital punishment.
- ☑ Corporal punishment.
- ☑ Mutilation.
- ☑ Imprisonment or incarceration.
- ☑ Fines.

What type of punishment is capital punishment?

Capital punishment, also known as the death penalty, is when a criminal is executed, usually for treason or very severe crimes. It is not a legal *(p.26)* punishment in Great Britain today.

What is corporal punishment?

Corporal punishment is the infliction of physical pain on the body.

What is mutilation as a punishment?

Mutilation was a severe form of punishment in the past. It would involve disfiguring parts of the criminal's body, such as cutting off a hand, ear or the nose, or even putting out the eyes.

What is imprisonment as a punishment?

Imprisonment involves holding criminals in captivity and keeping them entirely separate from the rest of the population.

What are fines as a punishment?

Fines are a demand for financial or other form of material payment from the criminal.

What was the purpose of punishment?

Punishments have 5 different purposes.

- ✅ Reform.
- ✅ Retribution.
- ✅ Deterrence.
- ✅ Removal.
- ✅ Humiliation.

What is reform as an aim of punishment?

Some punishments aim to reform the criminal, changing the person so they are no longer at risk of committing crime. This is sometimes called rehabilitation.

What is retribution as an aim of punishment?

Retribution is the notion a person should pay for what they did. It is about society having vengeance.

What is deterrence as an aim of punishment?

Historically, some punishments were severe and frightening enough to deter - or prevent - people from committing the same crimes in future.

What is removal as an aim of punishment?

Removal involves taking the criminal out of society so they can no longer cause a nuisance or threat. This might be through a temporary method such as imprisonment or a permanent one like the death penalty.

What is humiliation as an aim of punishment?

Some punishments in history would happen in public. This was to humiliate the offender, shaming them in front of others and ultimately deterring others from committing crimes.

DID YOU KNOW?

The point of punishments can change over time.

One of the harshest retributive punishments was being hung, drawn and quartered. This involved being strangled, castrated and disembowelled while still alive.

TRENDS IN ANGLO-SAXON CRIME

Anglo-Saxon attitudes to crime and punishment reflected life in isolated communities and a struggle for survival.

What was the Anglo-Saxon approach to crime?

Most Anglo-Saxons lived in small, isolated rural communities. Crime and punishment often reflected their lifestyle and poverty.

What were the most common crimes in Anglo-Saxon England?

There were 2 popular types of crime in Anglo-Saxon time:

- ✅ Most crimes involved the theft of money, food and/or belongings, all usually of low value. This was called petty theft.

Quizzes, amazing exam preparation tools and more at GCSEHistory.com

☑ Violent crimes accounted for a small minority of cases.

Who were the criminals in Anglo-Saxon England?

Any man aged 14 or over who tried to avoid trial and punishment *(p.19)* by running away from his community was known as an outlaw *(p.25)*.

DID YOU KNOW?

Anglo-Saxon kings would sometimes issue Codes of Law.
This might be to reinforce old laws, or introduce new ones.

ANGLO-SAXON LAW ENFORCEMENT

Anglo-Saxon law enforcement relied heavily on collective responsibility and the local community.

How did Anglo Saxons enforce the law?

Law enforcement *(p.26)* in Anglo-Saxon society relied heavily on the principle of collective responsibility.

What was the role of the victims in Anglo-Saxon law enforcement?

Victims of crime were expected to find the criminal themselves.

How did they catch criminals in Anglo-Saxon law enforcement?

The victim or witnesses were expected to call out to fellow villagers to assist in chasing the criminal. This was known as the hue and cry. If a person did not join in the chase the whole village would have to pay a heavy fine.

Who were the Anglo-Saxon law enforcement officials?

Shire reeves were appointed from the local community to make sure people followed the king's law *(p.26)*.

How did the Anglo-Saxon kings enforce the law?

There were 2 main ways the king enforced the law *(p.26)* in Anglo-Saxon England:

☑ He was responsible for the 'King's Peace', which meant the people of Anglo-Saxon England held him ultimately responsible for protecting them and providing justice.

☑ Only the king could make laws, which were issued as Codes of Law *(p.26)*. These might add new laws, or reinforce or change existing ones.

How was policing organised in Anglo-Saxon England?

Policing *(p.26)* duties in Anglo-Saxon England were divided between the local community and the king's men in 2 key ways:

☑ The shire reeve acted on behalf of the king to make sure people followed the law *(p.26)*.

☑ Local communities were divided into tithings to police *(p.26)* each other. A tithing was a group of ten people.

How did tithings enforce the law in Anglo-Saxon England?

Tithings enforced the law *(p.26)* in 3 different ways:

- ☑ The men of the tithing were responsible for the behaviour of everyone in the ten households.
- ☑ If someone saw a crime being committed, they had to raise a hue and cry by shouting so that anyone who heard could chase the criminal. Anyone who failed to do this had to pay a fine.
- ☑ If someone refused to join the fyrd, the whole tithing had to pay a fine.

DID YOU KNOW?

All men over the age of 12 joined the tithing.

ANGLO-SAXON TRIALS

Anglo-Saxon trials relied on oaths, compurgation and a jury system.

How did the Anglo-Saxons use trials?

When Anglo-Saxons were accused of a crime, they were taken to court to determine their guilt at trial.

What type of trials were used by the Anglo-Saxons?

Anglo-Saxons used 2 different types of trials to determine guilt.

- ☑ They used juries of local people to decide whether the accused was innocent or guilty.
- ☑ If they could not decide then the accused underwent trial by ordeal *(p.23)*.

How were oaths used in Anglo-Saxon trials?

There were 4 ways the practice of taking oaths was used in Anglo-Saxon trials.

- ☑ An oath would take place in public and the accused would swear their innocence before God.
- ☑ The accused could call upon oath helpers from their community to support their claims in court.
- ☑ If a jury felt the victim was more honest than the accused, they would swear an oath the accused was guilty.
- ☑ An accused could take an oath of innocence by asking a required number of people, usually twelve, to swear they believed the defendant. This oath was called compurgation.

What courts did Anglo-Saxons use for trials?

As Anglo-Saxon kings 4 different courts which dealt with different kinds of cases.

- ☑ The Royal Court was also known as the Witan. Here the king decided cases involving his lords and other serious crimes.
- ☑ Shire Courts were held in every shire or county and met twice a year to deal with serious cases such as murder. All landowners and a representative from each village were required to attend, and local noblemen acted as the judges.
- ☑ All freemen had to attend Hundred Courts, which were local and met each month. This was where they joined tithings and swore to keep the peace. It dealt with less serious cases.
- ☑ Private Courts dealt with people who had broken local rules, such as workers who hadn't done enough work on the lord's land or slaves who had tried to run away. The local landowner would be the judge.

Quizzes, amazing exam preparation tools and more at GCSEHistory.com

TRIALS BY ORDEAL

When in doubt, the Anglo-Saxons gave God the opportunity to reveal the guilt or innocence of the accused.

What was trial by ordeal?

In early medieval times, when the guilt of a criminal could not be decided, a trial by ordeal was held to allow God to determine whether or not an accused was guilty.

Which trials by ordeal did the Anglo-Saxons use?

The Anglo-Saxons used 4 main trials by ordeal.

- ☑ Trial by hot water.
- ☑ Trial by hot iron, often used for women accused of crimes.
- ☑ Trial by cold water, often used for serfs or other people of low status.
- ☑ Trial by consecrated (or blessed) bread, which was taken by priests.

Which trial by ordeal did the Normans introduce?

As well as the Anglo-Saxon trials by ordeal, the Normans used trial by combat.

How was combat used in the trial by ordeal?

Trial by combat was where the accused fought with the accuser until one of them was killed or unable to fight on. The loser was then hanged, as God had judged them to be guilty.

How was hot water used in the trial of ordeal?

For a trial by hot water, the accused had to plunge their hand into boiling water and have it bandaged for three days. If the burn healed well, this was seen as a sign God judged the person to be innocent.

How was hot iron used in a trial by ordeal?

In trial by hot iron, hot iron was used to burn the hand, which was bandaged for three days. If the burn healed well, this was seen as a sign God had found the person innocent.

How was cold water used in a trial of ordeal?

In trial by cold water, the accused had their arms tied and was thrown into a pond or river that had been blessed by a priest. Those who floated were found guilty as God had 'rejected' them, while those who sank were judged innocent and hauled up again.

How was blessed bread used in a trial of ordeal?

Trial by consecrated, or blessed, bread was taken by priests. He would first have to pray, asking that he be choked by the bread if he lied. If he did, it meant he was guilty.

 How were trials by ordeal conducted in Anglo-Saxon times?

There were 3 important procedures in the way the trials by ordeal were run.

- ☑ Because the trials were designed to allow God to decide on the guilt or innocence of the accused, a priest had to be present.
- ☑ The accused would often spend three days at a holy site or in a church or monastery before the trial, praying and fasting.
- ☑ The accused would attend mass before the trial.

DID YOU KNOW?

Trials by ordeal could be adjusted.

Trial by hot iron involved holding a piece of red-hot iron while walking a specified number of paces. The weight of the iron and the number of paces depended on the alleged crime.

ANGLO-SAXON PUNISHMENTS

The harshest punishments were usually given to repeat offenders.

 What punishments were there in Anglo-Saxon society?

The Anglo-Saxons used a variety of punishments in response to crime, including capital and corporal punishment *(p.19)*, as well as mutilation and humiliation.

 What was the punishment for murder in Anglo-Saxon England?

Criminals often had to pay compensation to their victims, called wergild or the 'blood price'. The level of fine was carefully worked out and set through the king's laws. This replaced the old system of blood feuds.

 Did the Anglo-Saxons use the death penalty as a punishment?

Serious crimes carried the death penalty, such as treason against the king or betraying a superior or lord.

 Did they use corporal punishment in Anglo-Saxon England?

Reoffenders faced corporal punishment *(p.19)*, which was the infliction of pain on the body. This included mutilation like cutting off a hand or the nose.

How did Anglo-Saxons punish minor crimes?

Less severe corporal punishments included the stocks or pillory. These were located outdoors and kept a criminal trapped by the arms, neck and ankles, sometimes for several days.

Did Anglo-Saxons have prisons as a form of punishment?

Prisons were rarely used in Anglo-Saxon society because they were expensive. They were only used for holding serious criminals before trial.

Why did the Anglo-Saxons punish criminals?

There were 3 main reasons why Anglo-Saxons punished criminals:

- ☑ They needed to maintain order in the social structure, and respect for the important lords.
- ☑ They needed to protect a society in which survival was already a struggle.
- ☑ The influence of the church meant some of their punishment *(p.19)* reflected a belief in redemption.

How did the Anglo-Saxons use retribution in their punishments?

Wergild was a form of retribution, and a sort of fine.

How did the Anglo-Saxons use deterrence in their punishments?

Capital and corporal punishments were intended to deter (stop) others from committing crimes. This was especially true of mutilation, with the disfigured criminal serving as a constant reminder of the consequences of crime.

How did the Anglo-Saxons use reform in their punishments?

The Anglo-Saxon church promoted mutilation as an alternative to the death penalty, as it gave the criminal an opportunity to reform.

How did the Anglo-Saxons use humiliation in their punishments?

The stocks and the pillory were used for public humiliation.

DID YOU KNOW?

The Anglo-Saxon church encouraged mutilation.

It saw mutilation as an opportunity for the criminal to reform and rehabilitate, as opposed to the finality of the death penalty.

OUTLAWS

Seeking to escape legal retribution, they lived outside society.

Who were outlaws?

Throughout medieval times, crime and punishment in England featured people known as outlaws - those who lived outside of the law *(p.26)*.

What were outlaws like?

Outlaws had 3 important traits:

- ☑ Outlaws were men who had broken the law *(p.26)*.
- ☑ They then escaped from their trial or punishment *(p.19)* and lived in remote areas, such as the forest.
- ☑ The female equivalent was known as a 'waived woman'.

How were outlaws treated?

There were 2 main ways of dealing with outlaws:

- ☑ Sometimes the shire reeve, or sheriff, was tasked with finding the outlaw.
- ☑ Anyone could assault, steal from or murder an outlaw without facing criminal charges.

> **DID YOU KNOW?**
>
> During the late Middle Ages, outlaw gangs based in the forest, such as the Folville Gang, terrorised their areas and attacked travellers.

TRENDS IN CRIME IN NORMAN ENGLAND

The Normans defined crimes in a similar way to the Anglo-Saxons, but protected their new invasion force by making more behaviours illegal.

What was the Norman attitude to crime?

William I believed crimes were committed against the King's Peace rather than against other people, and was therefore much harsher on criminals.

What impact did the Normans have on crime?

Medieval chroniclers say England was a safer and more law-abiding *(p.26)* place after the Norman conquest. However, this was out of fear rather than love for the Normans.

How did Norman language change crime and punishment?

The Normans primarily spoke French. They introduced many French and Latin words into the English language, many of them linked to the law *(p.26)*.

> **DID YOU KNOW?**
>
> **The amount paid as wergild in Norman times depended on the victim and the injury.**
>
> For example, at one point the life of a nobleman was worth 300 shillings, while the life of a serf was worth 40. The loss of a thumb cost 20 shillings and a broken nose cost 6.

CHANGES TO THE LAW IN NORMAN ENGLAND

Norman law featured a lot of continuity from the Anglo-Saxon system, but there were some additions.

What was the Norman legal system?

One of the main features of Norman government was the legal system. William I kept most of the Saxon system, but did introduce some important changes.

Quizzes, amazing exam preparation tools and more at GCSEHistory.com

How did Norman law enforcement work?

The Normans kept the Anglo-Saxon system of local community law enforcement and collective responsibility, with trials by ordeal run by the Church.

 What stayed the same in the Norman legal system?

When William became king he promised to keep the laws of Edward the Confessor. He did this for various reasons.

- ☑ The Saxon legal system was sophisticated and it worked. There was no need to change it.
- ☑ Keeping Saxon laws meant continuity and would help William's claim to be the legitimate king of England.
- ☑ Keeping Saxon laws removed a reason for the Saxon population to rebel against Norman rule.

 How did the Normans change the legal system?

Although he kept much of the Saxon legal system in place, William did make a few important changes.

- ☑ He introduced some new laws, in order to maintain Norman power in England.
- ☑ He introduced new courts, which increased the power of Norman lords over their lands.
- ☑ He made changes to the way criminals were punished, which helped to maintain Norman power and also made money for the king.
- ☑ The Normans centralised the system. Under the Saxons there had been many regional variations in the laws and legal system, so the Normans introduced uniformity throughout the country.
- ☑ Under the Normans, the language of the law became Norman-French. This was a disadvantage to the Saxons, most of whom did not speak the language.

 What new laws did the Normans introduce?

Although William I kept most of the existing Saxon laws, he did introduce some new ones to ensure the Normans kept their power and control.

- ☑ He introduced new laws, such as the murdrum fine, to protect his Norman followers against attacks by the Saxons.
- ☑ He introduced the forest laws to protect the land he set aside as his own hunting grounds.
- ☑ He introduced new laws on inheritance to prevent his lords' estates from being broken up. This helped his lords to consolidate and maintain their power.

 What was murdrum in the Norman legal system?

The murdrum fine was introduced by the Normans. If a Norman was killed, people in the local area had five days to produce the murderer. If they failed, they faced a large fine.

 How did the Normans enforce the law?

The Saxon system of law enforcement, which worked on the principle of collective responsibility, was effective. The Normans continued this.

- ☑ Normans continued the Anglo-Saxon tradition of constables and watchmen who were elected or appointed in towns. They kept the peace and enforced curfews.
- ☑ The tithing was kept, where groups of men guaranteed each other's good behaviour.
- ☑ The hue and cry remained and was raised whenever a crime was committed. Everyone was expected to help chase and catch the criminal or face a fine.

 How did trials work in the Norman legal system?

The Normans kept the Saxon methods of trying criminals. As evidence was sometimes difficult to produce, there were various ways to establish innocence or guilt.

- ✅ People would swear oaths in court about a person's guilt or innocence, based on their knowledge of the person. As oaths were religious rituals, people were expected to tell the truth or face God's punishment *(p.19)*.

- ✅ Trial by ordeal *(p.23)* was sometimes used. The Saxon ordeals included trial by cold water and trial by hot iron. The Normans also introduced trial by combat (or trial by battle).

 ## What were the courts in the Norman legal system?

Trials were held in the courts. The Normans kept most of the Saxon courts, but also introduced new ones.

- ✅ The King's Court dealt with royal pleas, including the most serious offences: murder, treason, arson, robbery and rape. The king would also hear appeals from the lower courts.

- ✅ The Shire Courts were supervised by the sheriff (or shire-reeve). These met regularly in each shire and made judgements on violent crime and theft. They also heard land disputes.

- ✅ The Hundred Courts were held monthly and supervised by a bailiff, who was appointed by the sheriff. These dealt with minor disputes that did not need to be heard by the sheriff himself.

- ✅ The Lord's Court (or honorial court) was introduced by the Normans. Lords could deal with their tenants, hearing criminal cases and disputes and also dealing with property transactions.

- ✅ The Manor Courts were held at village level. Each lord of the manor would deal with cases arising from day-to-day life.

- ✅ The Normans also introduced Church Courts. These dealt with religious and moral crimes, including adultery. Church courts were also reserved to try members of the Church for any crime.

What punishments were there in the Norman legal system?

Norman punishments tended to be harsher than under Saxon kings. They also provided revenue for the king which increased his wealth.

- ✅ If the accused was found innocent, the accuser was punished for making a false claim and had to pay a fine to both the king and the accused.

- ✅ Some lesser crimes such as theft or causing injury were settled by paying compensation to the victim. This was similar to the Saxon system.

- ✅ The Saxons had operated wergild for more serious crimes, where compensation was paid to the victim's family. Every freeman had a wergild price.

- ✅ Under the Normans, wergild declined. Serious offences were now punished by hanging or mutilation. The Normans were more inclined to use brutality and terror as a deterrent.

- ✅ Fines paid for more serious offences now went to the king rather than the victim's family.

DID YOU KNOW?

William I couldn't speak English.

He tried to learn, but apparently didn't really have the time.

NORMAN FOREST LAW

New laws were introduced for William's sporting grounds.

 ## What were the Royal Forests?

William kept a bigger area of land for himself ('demesne') than Edward the Confessor had previously. He turned a lot of land into the 'Royal Forests' - land reserved for hunting.

Why did William make the Royal Forests?

William created the Royal Forests because he really enjoyed hunting, particularly deer.

How did William create the Royal Forests?

William confiscated land from other land-holders, including the church, and evicted families from their homes.

What laws covered the Royal Forests?

Numerous laws were created to protect William's hunting grounds and the animals in them.

- ✅ Hunting on private land became a new crime, known as poaching *(p.57)*.
- ✅ Damage to the animals or vegetation was prohibited.
- ✅ It was an offence to take weapons or dogs into the forest.
- ✅ It was illegal for ordinary people to hurt the deer, even if the animals were damaging crops.

Why were the Royal Forests important?

The Royal Forests were significant in a number of ways.

- ✅ When William extended his area of land, he legitimised land-grabs being committed by other Normans and made them seem acceptable.
- ✅ It showed the power of the king was greater than the existing law *(p.26)*.
- ✅ Harsh punishments for poaching *(p.57)* demonstrated Norman ruthlessness.
- ✅ The Anglo-Saxon population began to resent the forests.
- ✅ The forest areas became another source of income for the king.

DID YOU KNOW?

Hunting was a dangerous sport.

William I's second son, Richard, his third son, William, and his grandson, Richard, were all killed while hunting in the Royal Forests.

TRENDS IN CRIME AND PUNISHMENT IN LATE MEDIEVAL ENGLAND

The later Middle Ages saw the introduction of more officials in law enforcement.

What was crime and punishment like in late medieval England?

Most Norman aspects of crime and punishment continued during the late medieval period in England, but there were some changes.

How did events in late medieval England affect crime and punishment?

There were 4 important events in late medieval England that affected crime and punishment.

- ✅ England was ruled by kings. Strong ones, such as Edward I and Henry II, tightened their hold on law and order, but weak kings were unable to control society well enough to prevent crime *(p.26)*.

- [✓] It's believed the Black Death of 1348-1351 may have killed up to two-thirds of the population. This led to massive social upheaval and the creation of several new crimes such as vagrancy.
- [✓] The Wars of the Roses, from 1455 to 1485, was a period of civil war that meant reduced control over individuals' behaviour, especially those who were powerful.
- [✓] From the end of the 1300s, a group of people called Lollards challenged the teachings of the Roman Catholic Church. This threatened the status quo of law and order.

How was crime defined in late medieval England?

During the late medieval period, 4 main crimes were redefined and others were introduced.

- [✓] In 1275, Edward I redefined 'felonies' in his Statutes of Winchester. This was updated to include rape and the theft of anything valued at more than 12d.
- [✓] In 1351, Parliament defined 'vagrancy' as a crime to prevent workers leaving their lord's land to seek better pay elsewhere.
- [✓] In 1351, Parliament redefined treason. High treason was against the king, while petty treason was against a master, husband or superior. Counterfeiting was also considered treason.
- [✓] Some manor courts in late medieval England began to convict people (usually women) of 'scolding'.

When was the late medieval period in England?

The late medieval period in England is generally described as circa 1100 to 1500.

What role did kings play in the crime and punishments of late medieval England?

Kings took a closer interest in laws, policing (p.26), trials and punishments in late medieval England in 4 main ways:

- [✓] At the Assize of Clarendon in 1166, King Henry II reorganised the system of courts to make it more efficient.
- [✓] Royal judges, called the Justices of Eyre, travelled around the country to hear cases.
- [✓] Keepers of the King's Peace were appointed by Richard I.
- [✓] Justices of the Peace were introduced by Edward III.

Who policed late medieval England?

There was no police (p.26) force in late medieval England and villagers had to raise the hue and cry to chase and catch criminals. However, new roles in law enforcement were introduced, while others became more important.

What policing roles were introduced in late Medieval England?

There were 5 key law enforcement (p.26) roles:

- [✓] Coroners.
- [✓] Constables.
- [✓] Watchmen.
- [✓] Sheriffs.
- [✓] Justices of the Peace.

Who were constables in late medieval England?

Leading villagers in late medieval times chose a constable to help with policing (p.26). They held the role for a year and it was unpaid. Their main responsibility was to keep the peace in their spare time and lead the hue and cry when necessary.

Who were watchmen in late medieval England?

In late medieval towns constables were helped by the watchmen. These were citizens who kept watch for crime during the night and handed over any suspected wrongdoers to the constable in the morning.

Who were coroners in late medieval England?

In the 1190s, the king introduced coroners. Their task was to enquire into all unnatural deaths with the help of a local jury.

Who were sheriffs in late medieval England?

If villagers failed to catch the criminal then the shire reeve, who became known as the sheriff, had the job of tracking miscreants down and imprisoning them.

Who were Keepers of the King's Peace in late medieval England?

In 1195, Richard I sent loyal knights to help control unruly areas. These became known as 'Keepers of the King's Peace'.

Who were Justices of the Peace in late medieval England?

In 1361, Edward III appointed 'good and lawful men' to keep the peace in all counties of England. These were Justices of the Peace, and acted as local magistrates.

DID YOU KNOW?

Murder rates in the late medieval period were high.

Historians say this was because people lived and worked closely with each other and had sharp farming tools to hand if they quarrelled. Poor medical understanding meant wounds could kill if they became infected. The murder figures also included suicides.

THE CHURCH AND THE LAW IN LATE MEDIEVAL ENGLAND

One law for the people, another for the clergy.

What was the role of the medieval Church in crime and punishment?

The Church played a central role in medieval law and order. This influence sometimes brought it into conflict with the king.

How could the medieval Church influence law and order?

The medieval Church had 4 main roles to play in law enforcement *(p.26)*.

- ☑ It oversaw trials by ordeal until these were formally ended by the pope in 1215.
- ☑ It dealt with a range of moral crimes.
- ☑ It offered benefit of clergy, which allowed criminal clergymen and other church workers to be tried by a more lenient Church court.
- ☑ It offered sanctuary, which was protection for criminals who claimed it.

How did the medieval Church come into conflict with the king over crime and punishment?

There are 4 important reasons why the Church came into conflict with the King.

- ☑ Henry II challenged the Church over its courts more than any other king.
- ☑ He believed Church courts were too lenient on criminals in the clergy because they never sentenced people to death.
- ☑ He disliked churchmen being outside his control when it came to law and order.

☑ He felt Church courts made law enforcement *(p.26)* less consistent across England.

What role did Becket play in law and order in the medieval Church?

King Henry II fell out with the Archbishop of Canterbury, Thomas Becket, over the issue of Church courts. Becket was brutally murdered by the king's men in 1170 and Henry was eventually forced to seek forgiveness.

Why was the medieval Church a problem to law and order?

In the eyes of King Henry II and some later kings, the continuing strong power and influence of the Church challenged royal authority and hindered effective justice.

How were medieval Church courts misused?

Church courts were misused in 4 key ways:

☑ Some criminals used the Church courts to try and avoid severe punishments.

☑ They would claim benefit of clergy as being tried in a Church court was far less likely to end in a sentence of death.

☑ Some shaved their hair into a tonsure to disguise themselves as churchmen.

☑ There was no way for the Church to check whether the accused belonged to the clergy or not.

How did sanctuary work in the medieval Church?

There were 4 ways sanctuary worked under the medieval Church:

☑ Anyone who claimed sanctuary was then protected by the Church and could not legally be removed by force.

☑ The criminal then had 40 days to decide whether to face trial or leave the country.

☑ Those who left had to go barefoot and carry a wooden cross. They were expected to board the first ship heading overseas.

☑ Sometimes they were escorted to the coast by guards, to protect them from vengeful citizens and ensure they left.

What was the 'benefit of clergy' in the medieval Church?

The church offered its workers 'benefit of clergy' if they were accused of a crime. It was essentially a way of allowing them to receive a more lenient punishment *(p.19)*.

How did the 'benefit of clergy' work in the medieval Church?

There were 5 main ways the benefit of clergy worked:

☑ Benefit of clergy allowed the accused to be tried in a Church court, which was more lenient and less likely to sentence them to death.

☑ This right was only meant for priests but could be claimed by anyone who worked in the Church.

☑ As there wasn't always a way to check whether the accused worked for the Church, its authorities introduced a test to make sure they were clergymen.

☑ The test involved reading a psalm from the Bible as generally only churchmen could read.

☑ The psalm was always Psalm 51, which led to criminals learning and reciting the verse from memory in order to claim benefit of clergy.

What was the 'neck verse' in medieval Church courts?

The Church asked the accused who claimed benefit of clergy to read a Bible verse to prove they were churchmen. It was always the same psalm, so those outside the clergy learned it by heart. It became known as the 'neck verse' because it helped them escape hanging.

What happened to trials by ordeal in the medieval Church?

Trials by ordeal were officially ended during the late medieval period.

When were the trials by ordeal ended by the medieval Church?

They were formally abandoned in 1215.

Who ended the trials by ordeal in the medieval Church?

Pope Innocent III banned church involvement in trials by fire and water.

Why were trials by ordeal abandoned by the medieval Church?

This was because the Church was becoming more rational and taking a greater interest in securing justice.

DID YOU KNOW?

Henry II was famous for his temper tantrums.

Apparently they caused his eyes to become bloodshot and red. He would fall to the floor until he calmed down!

THE EARLY MODERN CHURCH AND THE LAW

Religious instability in the early modern church led to changes to crime and punishment.

How much influence did the English Reformation have on crime and punishment?

The church remained highly influential in crime and punishment during the early modern period *(p.34)*, but experienced a time of instability and change.

How did English reformation affect the definition of crime?

Because religion influenced ideas about crime so heavily, the English Reformation led to a time during which definitions of crime changed rapidly.

What was the social impact of the English Reformation?

The English Reformation had 4 important social impacts.

- ☑ The religious upheaval of the English Reformation had a profound impact on early modern society *(p.34)*.
- ☑ It resulted in divisions in society according to belief.
- ☑ Protestants and Catholics accused each other of being in league with the devil.
- ☑ This helped increase public belief in evil and supernatural explanations for events.

How did the English Reformation affect law and order?

The English Reformation influenced law and order in 4 significant ways.

- ☑ The Church continued to play a direct role in crime and punishment during the early modern period *(p.34)*.
- ☑ Church courts remained in use during the early modern period *(p.34)*.
- ☑ They dealt with crimes committed by men of the Church and anyone that could claim benefit of clergy.

☑ However, as so many more people could read the neck verse by the 1600s, the law *(p.26)* was changed to prevent those accused of serious crimes from claiming benefit of clergy.

DID YOU KNOW?

The Reformation and the rise of Protestantism is often believed to have begun in 1517.

A German monk named Martin Luther nailed a list of errors that he saw in Roman Catholic teaching to the door of the church in Wittenberg. These were known as the '95 Theses'.

THE IMPACT OF THE EARLY MODERN PERIOD ON CRIME AND PUNISHMENT

Bigger cities meant more upheaval, more poverty - and new crimes.

❓ What was the early modern period?

This period saw many changes to society that are sometimes referred to as 'the Renaissance'. It affected crime and punishment in a number of ways.

⧖ When was the early modern period?

The early modern period is considered to be circa 1500-1700.

⚖ What was the population in the early modern period?

During the 16th and 17th centuries the population of England increased from about 3 million people in 1500 to some 5.1 million people in 1700.

⚖ What was the impact of the population rise in the early modern period?

The rise of the population in England in the early modern period had 3 important impacts.

☑ More people meant it was more difficult for some of them to find work.

☑ A bigger population meant prices rose.

☑ This led to greater poverty, which in turn had an impact on crime as some people struggled to survive.

⚖ How were the rich affected in the early modern period?

There were 3 ways the rich were affected in the early modern period.

☑ There were greater opportunities for trade and so there were more wealthy people.

☑ Many rich landowners wanted a bigger say in the way the country was run.

☑ They had a growing influence on the making of laws.

⚖ How were the poor affected in the early modern period?

There were 6 ways the poor were affected in the early modern period.

☑ Bad harvests and famine meant food prices rose throughout the 1500s.

☑ The growing population also led to a rise in food prices.

- ☑ The growth of the wool trade and the replacement of crops with animal farming meant there were fewer jobs available for farm labourers.
- ☑ The collapse of the wool trade in Europe in the later 1500s led to further job losses.
- ☑ Real wages fell by 60% during this period.
- ☑ The rise in poverty alongside a growth in wealth led to greater inequality. This presented more opportunities for crime.

How did towns change in the early modern period?

During the early modern period towns changed in 3 important ways.

- ☑ Overall, the urban population of Britain grew from about 10% in 1500 to around 20% in 1750.
- ☑ The population of London grew from around 50,000 people in 1500 to around 600,000 in 1700.
- ☑ Growing urban populations led to more crime, because towns offered more anonymity and there was a greater inequality of wealth between citizens.

What was the impact of newspapers in the early modern period?

The use of the printing press in the late 15th century impacted crime and punishment in 6 ways.

- ☑ London had its first printing press in the year 1476.
- ☑ More books, broadsheets and pamphlets started to appear and were more affordable.
- ☑ Pamphlets were often illustrated and might be read out to the illiterate.
- ☑ A favourite topic for pamphlets was crime, particularly witchcraft *(p.39)* and vagabondage *(p.38)*.
- ☑ This made it easier for people to share and access ideas about crime, and they became more aware of it.
- ☑ There was a market for broadsheets which attracted readers with tales of violent crimes. This made people believe there was more crime then there really was.

What war happened in the early modern period?

There was great instability at times during the early modern period.

- ☑ The greatest rebellion of all was the English Civil War (1642-49), in which Parliament fought and beat the king's forces.
- ☑ This resulted in the execution of King Charles I in 1649.
- ☑ At this time, many people felt the world had turned upside down, and they experienced insecurity and fear.
- ☑ Uprisings and rebellion were treated as crimes, but periods of instability also impacted the ability of society to effectively police *(p.26)* behaviour.

Why were there higher taxes in the early modern period?

Taxes rose in England during the early modern period for 3 important reasons.

- ☑ Governments were in greater need of money for wars and other expenses.
- ☑ As there was no income tax many other taxes were increased, including customs duties on imports.
- ☑ Rising taxes affected crime because they led to more poverty, but also because non-payment of tax was a further opportunity for crime.

What was early modern travel like?

There were 3 main reasons for the increased travel during the early modern period.

- ☑ In the Middle Ages, people had little freedom to move from place to place. By the 1500s these restrictions had been removed and there was increased travel between towns.
- ☑ Better roads helped the development of coaches, and horses became cheaper to buy.

☑ Travellers were more vulnerable to crime, however. They often travelled through isolated places and did not have the protection of a building.

What were trials and courts like in the early modern period?

Although trials showed great continuity during this period, there were some key changes.

☑ There was greater reliance on Justices of the Peace.

☑ By the end of the period there was recognition of habeas corpus *(p.38)*.

☑ There was greater use of juries.

☑ Witches underwent a trial by water in the early modern period, which was similar to the medieval trial by cold water.

What kind of courts were there in the early modern period?

There were a variety of courts at this time.

☑ All courts relied on a local jury.

☑ Royal judges visited each county twice a year to deal with the most serious cases. These were known as county assizes.

☑ Manor courts dealt with local, minor crimes such as selling underweight bread and drunkenness.

☑ Justices of the Peace dealt with minor crimes alone, but met up four times a year for the Quarter Sessions.

How did crime develop in in the early modern period?

Most crimes of the Middle Ages continued to be classed as such in the early modern period, but there were also new ones and some grew in importance to society.

What new crimes were there in the early modern period?

Changes to society in the early modern period meant vagabondage *(p.38)* became an important new crime.

Which crimes became more important in the early modern period?

Because of changes to early modern society, some crimes became more important than ever. These included:

☑ Witchcraft *(p.39)*.

☑ Treason.

How did the public view crime in the early modern period?

Despite the fall in crime in the late 1600s, most people believed crime was increasing. This was due to broadsheet publications which attracted readers with tales of violent crimes, and religious protests and rebellions which made people feel insecure.

What was policing like in the early modern period?

Policing *(p.26)* in the early modern period was much the same as during the Middle Ages, with few developments.

Which policing methods were similar in medieval times and the early modern period?

There were 5 aspects of policing *(p.26)* in the early modern period that remained the same as in the Middle Ages.

☑ Tithings and the hue and cry still existed in smaller communities.

☑ They were less effective in towns where there were more people.

☑ The constable was expected to lead the hue and cry.

☑ Parish constables remained the main defence against crime, dealing with everyday matters such as begging without a licence.

☑ They were expected to take charge of suspects and make sure they were held in prison until their trial.

How did policing change in the early modern period?

There were 6 important changes in policing *(p.26)* in early modern period.

- ✅ Constables were employed in larger towns to patrol the streets day and night. They were poorly paid and often of little use. Their duties included arresting drunks and vagabonds.
- ✅ Sergeants were employed in towns to enforce market regulations. They weighed goods and collected fines if traders behaved badly.
- ✅ People were expected to deal with crime themselves. If someone was robbed it was their responsibility to get an arrest warrant from a magistrate, track down the criminals and deliver them to the constable.
- ✅ Rewards were offered for the arrest of particular criminals, usually for more serious crimes. The rewards involved could be very high - even equivalent to a year's income for a middle-class family.
- ✅ Thief-takers made their living from tracking down criminals and collecting rewards. They were often former criminals themselves and would set up innocent victims, tricking them into crime.
- ✅ The army was used to put down protests or other riots. This was unpopular with the public as it seemed the government was simply overpowering the people and ignoring their concerns.

> ### DID YOU KNOW?
>
> **Women who were found guilty of treason were burned instead of being hanged, drawn and quartered.**
>
> This was because their clothes would have to be removed to cut their bodies open, and such nudity would be immoral.

THE DEVELOPING ROLE OF JPS IN THE EARLY MODERN PERIOD

Edward III described them as 'good and lawful men'.

? What were Justices of the Peace?

Justices of the Peace were introduced in medieval times, but the Tudors developed their role further.

 What did Justices of the Peace do?

Some important duties performed by Justices of the Peace were:

- ✅ Being responsible for making decisions about criminals.
- ✅ As they were magistrates, they made decisions about petty criminals on their own.
- ✅ Four times a year they would meet *(p.74)* with other JPs in the county at events called the Quarter Sessions.
- ✅ At the Quarter Sessions, JPs would judge more serious cases and could even decide to execute criminals.

 Who could become a Justice of the Peace?

The role was unpaid, so people who worked as JPs had to be rich enough to support themselves. They were often leading landowners and wealthy, educated citizens.

THE INTRODUCTION OF HABEAS CORPUS

'Habeas corpus' translates from the Latin as 'You have the body'.

What is habeas corpus?

Habeas corpus represented a big change in criminal law *(p.26)*.

What does habeas corpus mean?

Habeas corpus means 'you have the body'.

When was habeas corpus passed?

The Habeas Corpus Act was passed in 1679.

What rights did the Habeas Corpus Act give?

Habeas Corpus Act gave 5 important rights.

- ☑ The act improved the rights of citizens and those who were arrested.
- ☑ It prevented the authorities from locking a person up indefinitely without charging them with a crime.
- ☑ Anyone who was arrested had to appear in court within a certain time or be released.
- ☑ People no longer had to fear being seized and locked up without a trial.
- ☑ However, governments still sometimes made up evidence at trial as an excuse to lock up their critics.

VAGABONDAGE

A new crime - that of being poor and homeless.

What was vagabondage?

Vagabondage was an important new crime in the 1500s - that of being homeless, poor and unemployed.

Quizzes, amazing exam preparation tools and more at GCSEHistory.com

Who were vagabonds?

There were 4 different types of vagabonds.

- ✅ Vagabonds were beggars, tramps and vagrants who wandered the country without a settled job.
- ✅ Some vagabonds were soldiers who had been demobilised.
- ✅ Most were poor and unemployed people moving to a new town or village looking for work.
- ✅ Some vagabonds exhibited criminal behaviour, but not all.

Why were people worried about vagabonds?

There were several reasons why people worried about vagabonds:

- ✅ During the 1500s, concern over vagabonds increased.
- ✅ Most people did not object to helping the genuine poor, such as those who could not work because they were old or sick.
- ✅ However, people felt that idleness, or laziness, was wrong. Puritan religion taught that everyone should work hard to avoid acts of sin.
- ✅ Vagabonds were blamed for many crimes such as thefts, assaults and murders.
- ✅ Many people were worried about the cost. Each village and town raised poor-rates to help the genuine poor of their own parish. Local people did not want to spend their money supporting the poor or idle from another parish.
- ✅ Pamphlets and books warned about the dangers of vagabonds. These were widely read and as popular as detective novels are today.
- ✅ Vagabonds travelled from area to area, but people were naturally suspicious of strangers to their parish (local area).

DID YOU KNOW?

There were thought to be many different types of vagabonds.

Thomas Harman wrote a book in 1567 that identified 23 different sorts of vagabonds. These included the 'Counterfeit Crank' and the 'Doxy'.

WITCHCRAFT

It was believed witches were in league with the devil.

What was witchcraft?

Witchcraft was a crime that grew in importance during the early modern period *(p.34)*. It was the offence of working with the devil and using magic to damage the lives of others.

How was witchcraft dealt with in medieval times?

Although there had been accusations of witchcraft in the Middle Ages, these were dealt with by the more lenient Church courts and were not common.

How did the Tudors react to witchcraft?

The Tudors react to witchcraft in 5 important ways.

- ✅ Under the Tudors, laws against witchcraft became much harsher.
- ✅ In 1542, under Henry VIII, the law *(p.26)* changed and witchcraft became a criminal offence.

- ☑ Queen Elizabeth I introduced tough laws against witches.
- ☑ Times of uncertainty and unrest, such as the Reformation or the Gunpowder Plot *(p.49)*, caused the number of accusations of witchcraft to increase.
- ☑ King James I was a keen witch hunter. In 1597 he wrote about his views on witches in a book called Demonologie.

What did James I say about witchcraft?

There are 2 main facts to note about King James I and witchcraft:

- ☑ James I was very interested in witchcraft.
- ☑ He wrote a book called 'Demonologie' in 1597 before he became King of England about witchcraft that even set out how to conduct a witch trial.

What impact did James I have on witchcraft?

James I had 3 main effects on witchcraft:

- ☑ His book, Demonologie, encouraged witch hunting.
- ☑ It made suggestions for witch trials.
- ☑ It suggested children could be used as witnesses in witch trials, even though this was not accepted practice in criminal law *(p.26)*.

Who made accusations of witchcraft?

Most accusations of witchcraft were cases of ordinary villagers using another person as a scapegoat when something went wrong, like an illness or spoiled crops.

How many people were executed for witchcraft?

Throughout the 16th and 17th centuries up to 1,000 people were executed as witches, most of them women.

When did concern over witchcraft end?

The last witchcraft trial took place in 1717. The final law *(p.26)* saying witchcraft was a crime was repealed in 1736.

Why did they stop prosecuting witches?

Five reasons accusations of witchcraft had declined by 1700 were:

- ☑ The Enlightenment had begun and it was a time of increasingly rational thinking.
- ☑ The Royal Society was established in 1660, supported by the king. It advocated modern scientific methods and helped change people's thinking.
- ☑ While the belief in witches didn't disappear, educated people (who were usually the judges) were less likely to believe charges of witchcraft.
- ☑ People were becoming increasingly prosperous. This reduced tensions in the villages. The rich helped the poor more and it's likely there were fewer requests for help.
- ☑ The political and social instability caused by religious changes and the Civil War gradually eased.

What happened to witches in the early modern period?

There were 5 ways the wiches were tried in the early modern period *(p.34)*.

- ☑ Witches underwent a trial by water in the early modern period *(p.34)*.
- ☑ This was similar to the trials by ordeal in medieval times.
- ☑ The accused had their hands bound and were lowered into the water by rope.
- ☑ It was believed the innocent would sink and the guilty would float.
- ☑ If they floated, they would be examined for the 'Devil's mark' as final proof of witchcraft.

Quizzes, amazing exam preparation tools and more at GCSEHistory.com

HERESY

If you challenged the Church, you risked being accused of heresy.

What was heresy?

Heresy was the crime of challenging the accepted teachings of the Church.

Why did heresy change?

Heresy changed in 3 ways.

- ✅ Heresy became more important.
- ✅ From the 1500s, heresy was often linked to treason because of changes to the Church in England.
- ✅ As the role of the crown and the Church became more closely linked under Henry VIII, it became more difficult to distinguish treason and heresy from each other.

Why did heresy become a more serious crime?

From 1534, refusing to follow the state religion was an offence against the state as well as a religious offence.

THE RELATIONSHIP BETWEEN HERESY AND TREASON IN THE EARLY MODERN PERIOD

As the roles of church and state became more closely linked, so heresy and treason became intertwined.

What was the relationship between heresy and treason in the early modern period?

From around 1400 onwards, the issues of treason and heresy *(p.41)* became more closely linked.

How did the relationship between heresy and treason change?

The relationship between heresy *(p.41)* and treason changed in 3 key ways.

- ☑ Between 1400 and 1700, heresy *(p.41)* and treason became more entwined and were harder to tell apart.
- ☑ From the 15th century onwards, the roles of the Church and the state became more intertwined, which had an effect when it came to dealing with cases of heresy *(p.41)*.
- ☑ In the 16th century, changes to the Church meant any opposition to it could also be considered treason against the crown.

Why was heresy linked with treason in the early modern period?

There were 3 main reasons why heresy *(p.41)* was linked with treason in the early modern period *(p.34)*:

- ☑ Changes to English society and religion, particularly in the 16th century, caused a stronger link to grow between treason and heresy *(p.41)*.
- ☑ At the beginning of the 15th century, the king's men were given the job of carrying out punishments for heresy *(p.41)*.
- ☑ During the English Reformation *(p.33)*, the relationship between the Church and the throne became closer. This meant heresy *(p.41)* could be interpreted as treason and vice versa.

How did Henry VIII influence the relationship between treason and heresy?

There were 4 key ways in which Henry VIII influenced the relationship between treason and heresy *(p.41)*:

- ☑ Henry's actions in the English Reformation *(p.33)* led to more prosecutions for treason and heresy *(p.41)*.
- ☑ Under the Act of Supremacy in 1534, Henry became head of the church as well as head of the state. This meant anyone who disagreed with his religion could be accused of treason.
- ☑ Henry executed some Protestants as heretics during his reign.
- ☑ Many Catholics who protested against his changes to the English Church were executed as traitors.

How did Mary I influence the relationship between treason and heresy?

England rejoined the Roman Catholic Church under Queen Mary I. Almost 300 Protestants were burned as heretics.

How did Elizabeth I influence the relationship between treason and heresy?

Under Elizabeth, the relationship between treason and heresy *(p.41)* became even more complicated in 3 ways:

- ☑ Elizabeth separated the Church from Rome once again and became its governor.
- ☑ Under the Act of Uniformity of 1559, people who refused to go to Elizabeth's Church could be accused of the crime of recusancy and fined.
- ☑ In 1570 the pope excommunicated Elizabeth and declared her an enemy of the Roman Catholic Church. From that point onwards, Elizabeth considered people who followed Catholic beliefs to be traitors.

DID YOU KNOW?

Women could be found guilty of 'petty treason'.

This was the crime of plotting against or harming someone who was seen as their superior, such as a husband or master.

Quizzes, amazing exam preparation tools and more at GCSEHistory.com

THE PURITANS AND THE LAW

Under the Puritans, Christmas Day was replaced by spending the second Tuesday of every month in fasting and prayer.

 How did the Puritans define crime?

During the 1600s, a strongly Puritan parliament defined more sins as crimes, and law and order became more focused on moral crimes.

 How did Puritan beliefs influence their view of crime?

Puritan beliefs influenced their view of crime in 3 ways:

- ☑ Puritans were radical Protestants.
- ☑ They believed people should stay focused on a godly life, rather than a worldly one. Activities that were too enjoyable were seen as taking focus away from God and were therefore sinful.
- ☑ The Puritans wanted a society which made people fit for Heaven. They therefore viewed sinful behaviour as criminal.

 Why were the Puritans able to change what was defined as a crime?

There were 5 reasons why Puritans were able to change what was defined as a crime:

- ☑ The growing power of the Puritans meant they were in a position to define crimes under law *(p.26)* for some of the 1600s.
- ☑ From the beginning of the 17th century there were increasing numbers of Puritans, which gave their ideas more influence.
- ☑ Many members of Parliament were Puritans, which meant they had the power to make laws.
- ☑ During the Civil War and afterwards, during the Protectorate, the Puritan government had the power to impose their beliefs through law *(p.26)*.
- ☑ The Puritans wanted a society in which people lived holy lives and became fit for heaven. They therefore viewed sinful behaviour as criminal.

 Why did the Puritans see some leisure activities as crimes?

There were 2 reasons why the Puritans viewed some leisure activities as crimes:

- ☑ This was partly because they believed enjoyment and fun were a distraction from God.
- ☑ It was also because some leisure activities, such as the theatre or sports, might lead to people committing further sins such as drinking or fighting in the crowds.

 What did the Puritans consider to be crimes?

There were 7 behaviours the Puritans thought were criminal:

- ☑ Sports such as bear-baiting, cock-fighting and horse-racing were banned.
- ☑ Theatres in London were closed.
- ☑ In some areas, make-up was banned for women.
- ☑ Sunday was considered a day of rest, so anything considered to be work was banned.
- ☑ Festivals such as May Day, Whitsun, Easter and Christmas were banned on the grounds that they weren't fully religious festivals, and were therefore blasphemous.
- ☑ In 1650, swearing became a crime punishable with a fine.
- ☑ Also from 1650, adultery was punishable by death.

Did the Puritans stop any actions from being a crime?

The Puritans did decriminalise some religious behaviour and gave people more religious freedom. For example, recusancy was no longer a crime.

 Why did the Puritans stop influencing what was considered a crime?

The Puritan regime ended in 1660 when King Charles II was restored to the throne of England. He decriminalised many moral crimes and the people of England loved him for it.

DID YOU KNOW?

The Puritans attempted to make Christian festivals such as Christmas, Easter and Pentecost illegal.

Instead, they introduced a new holiday on the second Tuesday of every month. However, as people were supposed to spend it in prayer and fasting, they didn't consider it an adequate substitute.

THE ROLE OF THE EARLY MODERN CONSTABLE

The early modern period saw additional duties added to the role of constable.

 What was the early modern constable?

A constable was a law enforcement *(p.26)* officer that had existed in medieval towns, but in the early modern period *(p.34)* the role was expanded.

 What were the duties of the early modern constable?

During the early modern period *(p.34)* the constable had 4 important duties:

- ✅ In larger towns they were employed to patrol the streets day and night.
- ✅ They did not track down criminals themselves, but took charge of them until trial.
- ✅ They were expected to lead the hue and cry.
- ✅ They were expected to catch vagabonds and petty criminals, and to carry out corporal punishments on them.

 What was the status of the early modern constable?

Constable was a relatively low-status role. They were paid badly in return for undertaking a wide range of tasks.

DID YOU KNOW?

The role of a constable grew in the early modern period.

They were responsible for cleaning the roads, collecting some taxes and whipping vagabonds.

Quizzes, amazing exam preparation tools and more at GCSEHistory.com

JUSTICES OF THE PEACE AND LAW ENFORCEMENT

JPs were responsible for enforcing more than 300 laws by the year 1600.

 How did Justices of the Peace in the early modern period enforce the law?

During the early modern period *(p.34)*, JPs *(p.37)* were given more and more responsibility for law enforcement *(p.26)*.

 How did the role of Justices of the Peace in law enforcement expand in the early modern period?

The role of Justices of the Peace in law enforcement *(p.26)* expanded in 2 important ways.

- ☑ By 1600, they were responsible for enforcing over 300 laws.
- ☑ By the 1600s, JPs *(p.37)* were complaining their role was too large and included too many jobs for them to carry it out properly.

 What did Justices of the Peace do to enforce the law in the early modern period?

Under the Tudors, the role of the JP in law enforcement *(p.26)* grew to include 6 important roles:

- ☑ Checking bridges for safety and supervising the building of roads.
- ☑ Licensing ale-houses.
- ☑ Managing and collecting poor relief.
- ☑ Managing the Houses of Correction.
- ☑ Arresting vagrants.
- ☑ Regulating local sport.

DID YOU KNOW?

By 1600, Justices of the Peace were complaining about having too much to do

An instruction manual, written for JPs by William Lombarde in 1581, had more than 600 pages!

THE EARLY MODERN SHERIFF

A role on the decline - sheriffs lost some of their authority in the early modern period.

 How did the role of the sheriff change in the early modern period?

During the early modern period *(p.34)*, the sheriff's role and status changed.

 What happened to the role of the sheriff in early modern times?

During the early modern period *(p.34)*, the role of sheriff lost some authority. Sheriffs were less powerful or important than the Justices of the Peace.

 What did the early modern sheriff do?

During this time period, sheriffs were made responsible for running county gaols.

THIEF-TAKERS

Thief-takers provided mercenary law enforcement - and sometimes added to crime.

What were thief-takers?

Thief-takers were mercenaries who tracked down criminals and stolen goods for the reward of money.

Why were thief-takers part of law enforcement?

There were 3 main reasons why thief-takers were used as part of law enforcement *(p.26)*:

- ✅ Thief-takers were hired by victims of crime, who were responsible for catching the criminal themselves.
- ✅ They were sometimes criminals who stole the goods first before claiming the money for their return.
- ✅ Criminal thief-takers sometimes used their role to inform on rival criminal gangs.

THE ROLE OF VICTIMS OF CRIME IN THE EARLY MODERN PERIOD

The victims of crime were often responsible for tracking down those responsible themselves.

What was the role of crime victims in law enforcement in the 1700s?

If they wanted justice, victims of crime in early modern England were expected to play a role in catching the criminal.

What did early modern victims of crime have to do?

Early modern victims of crime had 3 key tasks to perform if they wanted justice:

- ✅ They had to get a warrant from the local Justice of the Peace *(p.37)*.
- ✅ They had to track down the criminal.
- ✅ They had to deliver the criminal to the constable for trial and sentencing.

Quizzes, amazing exam preparation tools and more at GCSEHistory.com

What solutions were found by victims of crime to catch criminals in early modern England?

The victims of crime in early modern England used 3 key methods to deal with crime:

- ☑ They offered rewards for the capture of the criminal or the return of stolen goods.
- ☑ They might hire thief-takers to catch the criminal for them.
- ☑ Traders in big towns might hire beadles to protect their premises.

DID YOU KNOW?

In early modern times, wealthy people were more able to afford protection from crime.

As well as hiring law enforcement to solve or prevent crimes committed against them, wealthy townspeople might also hire people to take their place for their turn as a watchman.

THE ROLE OF THE ARMY IN EARLY MODERN LAW ENFORCEMENT

The army was used as a last resort in early modern law and order.

 How was the army used in law enforcement?

The army was sometimes used in early modern law enforcement *(p.26)* to deal with large-scale disorder, such as big protests or riots.

 What was the reaction to the use of the army in early modern law enforcement?

The use of the army in law enforcement *(p.26)* was very unpopular. People saw it as the government forcing control on them.

DID YOU KNOW?

People disliked the use of the army in law and order.

When the first government police force was introduced in 1829, members were deliberately given a blue uniform to contrast with army uniforms, which at the time were red.

TRENDS IN EARLY MODERN PUNISHMENT

A focus on retribution gradually gave way to deterrence in early modern punishments.

 What punishments were used in the early modern times?

Many punishments in the early modern period *(p.34)* were the same as those of the medieval period. Some new ones were introduced, such as transportation.

What were the punishment trends in the early modern period?

There were 3 main changes in the early modern period *(p.34)* from the medieval period:

- ☑ Greater retribution and deterrence were shown with the increasing use of gory and painful death sentences, such as burning or hanging, drawing and quartering.
- ☑ The use of capital punishment *(p.19)* increased with the use of the Bloody Code *(p.63)*.
- ☑ Although harsh, the use of transportation was a less permanent method of removal than the death penalty.

How were vagabonds punished in the early modern period?

Throughout the 16th century, the government took 7 different measures against vagabonds:

- ☑ At the start of the early modern period *(p.34)*, vagabonds and vagrants were punished under a 1495 law *(p.26)* which ordered them to spend three days in the stocks before being sent back to their home parish.
- ☑ In 1531, a new law *(p.26)* stated that vagabonds should be 'whipped until their bodies were bloody' before being sent home.
- ☑ After 1547, the first offence would lead to two years of slavery. Second offences would lead to slavery for life or execution.
- ☑ From 1572, the first offence would lead to whipping and the burning of an ear. Second offences would lead to execution.
- ☑ In 1593, the 1572 Act was repealed as it was seen as too harsh.
- ☑ From 1598, vagrants were whipped and sent home. If they did not mend their ways they could be sent to a House of Correction, be banished from the country or executed.
- ☑ In 1601, Elizabeth's Poor Law provided more comprehensive care for the poor.

How were heretics punished in the early modern period?

The punishment *(p.19)* for heresy *(p.41)* was being burned at the stake for men, or beheading for women and members of the nobility.

How were traitors punished in the early modern period?

There were 4 main ways traitors were punished in the early modern period *(p.34)*:

- ☑ The punishment *(p.19)* for treason was hanging, drawing and quartering for men, or burning for women.
- ☑ This was a punishment *(p.19)* for treason from later medieval times but it became more common in the early modern period *(p.34)*.
- ☑ Criminals would be hanged until near death. Their intestines would then be pulled out, and their body cut into four pieces.
- ☑ Women weren't hanged, drawn and quartered because it would involve nudity. Instead, women who were guilty of petty treason or counterfeiting were burned to death.

How were witches punished in the early modern period?

Once someone was proved to be a witch they were executed, often by hanging.

What forms of corporal punishment existed in the early modern period?

There were 4 main methods of corporal punishment *(p.19)* which continued to be used in the Early Modern Period *(p.34)*.

- ☑ Pillory.
- ☑ Stocks.
- ☑ Whipping.
- ☑ Ducking stools.

DID YOU KNOW?

Local courts developed some interesting punishments for minor crimes.

The 'scold's bridle' was sometimes used for women who were seen as too angry or nagging too much. It was a heavy frame attached around the head, with a metal spike to hold down the tongue.

DUCKING STOOLS

The ducking stool was a local variation when it came to punishing petty and minor crimes.

What were ducking stools?

Ducking stools were wooden contraptions onto which a person was tied. They would then be repeatedly dunked in the local pond or river.

Who was punished with a ducking stool?

Ducking stools were popular as punishment *(p. 19)* for women who argued with or disobeyed their husband.

When were ducking stools used?

Although versions of the ducking stool had been used in the later Middle Ages, they became more popular in the early modern period *(p. 34)*.

DID YOU KNOW?

Repeated duckings could prove fatal, as the criminal might suffer from shock or drowning.

CASE STUDY: THE GUNPOWDER PLOT

An act of treason that reflected religious tensions of the time.

What was the Gunpowder Plot of 1605?

In 1605 a group of Catholics plotted, but failed, to blow up King James I and his ministers at the opening of Parliament.

Why did Catholics plot against the government in the Gunpowder Plot?

Catholics plotted against the government in the Gunpowder Plot for 4 important reasons:

- ☑ The Gunpowder Plot was a result of Catholic disappointment in the actions of James I.
- ☑ When James I became king in 1603, many Catholics were hopeful they would be allowed to worship more freely.
- ☑ However, many powerful members of James's council were strongly anti-Catholic.
- ☑ Laws against Catholics were tightened and more harshly enforced.

What was the plan of the Gunpowder Plot?

There were 4 important facts to note about the Gunpowder Plot:

- ☑ The Gunpowder Plotters wanted to take advantage of new explosive technology by using gunpowder.
- ☑ The plan was hatched by Robert Catesby.
- ☑ He wanted to blow up the Houses of Parliament and, in the ensuing confusion, lead a Catholic rebellion and place James's daughter, Elizabeth, on the throne.
- ☑ One of the 13 plotters, Guy Fawkes, filled a vault beneath Parliament with 36 barrels of gunpowder, enough to destroy the building and everyone in it.

How were those involved in the Gunpowder Plot discovered?

There were 4 important reason the plotters of Gunpowder Plot were discovered:

- ☑ A leak in the rebel group led to the discovery of the plot.
- ☑ An anonymous letter warned Lord Monteagle not to attend the opening of Parliament as it would 'receive a mighty blow'.
- ☑ He took the letter straight to Robert Cecil - the king's chief minister.
- ☑ The vaults beneath Parliament were then searched and Fawkes was caught and arrested.

What happened to the plotters in the Gunpowder Plot?

The Gunpowder Plotters came to a violent end in 3 main ways:

- ☑ Fawkes was tortured until he revealed the names of the other plotters and signed a confession.
- ☑ The rest of the plotters had escaped. However, government soldiers tracked them down, and Catesby and a number of the other plotters were killed.
- ☑ The rest were returned to London, where they were found guilty and sentenced to be hanged, drawn and quartered.

What were the long-term consequences of the Gunpowder Plot?

There were 6 main long-term consequences of the plot:

- ☑ In 1605, the Thanksgiving Act ordered that the events of 5th November should be commemorated each year.
- ☑ Catholics were banned from working in the legal *(p.26)* profession or becoming officers in the armed forces.
- ☑ Catholics would be restricted from voting, becoming MPs, or owning land.
- ☑ They were also banned from voting in any elections until 1829.
- ☑ In 1606, a law *(p.26)* called the Popish Recusants Act forced Catholics to take an oath of allegiance to the English crown.
- ☑ They were also forced to take part in Church of England services and rituals, or pay fines.

DID YOU KNOW?

The Gunpowder Plotters came from a long tradition of resistance to Protestantism.

Robert Catesby was expelled from university for refusing to swear allegiance to the Protestant church. His father was imprisoned twice for refusing to give up his Catholic faith.

Quizzes, amazing exam preparation tools and more at GCSEHistory.com

CASE STUDY: MATTHEW HOPKINS

Matthew Hopkins was a mysterious figure, self-styled as 'Witchfinder General' during the turbulence of the English Civil War.

Who was Matthew Hopkins?

Matthew Hopkins was a young lawyer from Essex. In the 1640s he became known as the Witchfinder General due to his 'ability' to spot witches.

What did Matthew Hopkins do?

Between 1645 and 1647, Matthew Hopkins led a witch hunt in the east of England. An unprecedented number of accusations of witchcraft *(p.39)* were made, and 250 cases of witchcraft came before the authorities in East Anglia.

How did Matthew Hopkins start the witch hunts?

Starting in the small town of Manningtree in Essex, Hopkins and his assistant, John Stearne, began searching East Anglia for witches.

What did Matthew Hopkins do in Manningtree?

In Manningtree, Hopkins named 36 women as witches and collected evidence against them. He charged them with using harmful magic against their neighbours or their neighbours' livestock.

Who did Matthew Hopkins accuse of witchcraft?

The majority of women accused by Hopkins were old and poor, the most vulnerable people in their village.

What methods did Matthew Hopkins' use?

Hopkins used 4 key methods of searching for evidence of witchcraft *(p.39)* as he investigated his suspects:

- ☑ He exhausted his suspects by keeping them standing and forcing them to walk.
- ☑ He also weakened their resistance by keeping them awake for days at a time. Exhausted and worn down, many confessed.
- ☑ If a mouse, fly or spider found its way into the room, Hopkins claimed it was a 'familiar', a creature created by the devil to do the witch's bidding.
- ☑ Any scar, boil or spot was regarded as proof of a 'devil's mark'. These were not difficult to find as a lifetime of poor diet and hardship usually left marks on people's bodies.

How successful was Matthew Hopkins?

Hopkins' so-called success at unmasking witches led to other areas of the country engaging him to rid them of witches.

Why did Matthew Hopkins lead witch hunts?

Hopkins charged for his services, demanding a fee for his time plus expenses. He might have also been motivated by a desire for fame or a genuine fear of witchcraft *(p.39)*.

Did Matthew Hopkins accuse any men of witchcraft?

There were cases of men being accused of being witches too. An 80-year-old local vicar was accused and made to undergo trial by water in the castle moat. He was found guilty and hanged.

Why did Matthew Hopkins stop hunting for witches?

There is no mention of Hopkins in official records after 1647. It is believed he most likely died from an illness.

What were the results of Matthew Hopkins' witch hunts?

Between 1645 and 1647, East Anglia witnessed at least 100 executions for witchcraft *(p.39)*, possibly more. Nineteen of these victims were women from Manningtree.

 What did Matthew Hopkins call himself?

He went by the title "Witchfinder General".

DID YOU KNOW?

Hopkins' arrests had a devastating effect.

Of the 36 Manningtree residents arrested for witchcraft, 19 were hanged. Nine died of gaol fever, 6 remained in gaol and only one was set free - in return for accusing other people of witchcraft.

THE IMPACT OF INDUSTRIAL SOCIETY ON CRIME AND PUNISHMENT

Industrialisation had an impact on the nature of crime, and on attitudes towards it.

? **What was the industrial period in Britain?**

The industrial period roughly refers to the 18th and 19th centuries. Britain experienced more social and economic change during this period than at any previous time. This had an effect on crime, punishment *(p.19)* and policing *(p.26)*.

 How did urbanisation affect industrial Britain?

The location of the population changed in 3 dramatic ways during the industrial age:

- ☑ In 1750 there were 9.5 million people, mostly living in villages.
- ☑ By 1900 the population had risen to 41.5 million and people mainly lived in towns and cities.
- ☑ Bigger cities meant more crime, as they were more anonymous and there were more opportunities for crime.

 How did population growth affect crime in industrial Britain?

The growth of the population affected crime rates in the industrial age in 2 key ways:

- ☑ The population of England increased by more than 100% in the 19th century.
- ☑ This meant crime increased as there were more potential criminals and more potential victims.

 What were working practices like in industrial Britain?

Changes to working practices also led to 3 key changes in patterns of crime:

- ☑ During the 18th century, most people made a living from farm work.
- ☑ By 1900, most found employment in workshops or factories in towns and cities.
- ☑ People were more likely to work near stores of valuable goods, which made theft easier. There were also more opportunities to commit white-collar crimes, such as fraud *(p.92)*.

 Was there democracy in industrial Britain?

Voting and the electorate changed dramatically during the industrial period in 4 main ways:

- ☑ By the mid-18th century, only 1 in every 8 men could vote.
- ☑ By 1885, 2 in 3 men had this right.
- ☑ Governments therefore began to make improvements to housing and health in order to win votes from ordinary people.
- ☑ This also had an impact on the laws governments made regarding crime and punishment.

What effect did poor harvests have on industrial Britain?

Poor harvests had less impact on people, as food could be imported from other countries more easily.

What effect did people travel in industrial Britain?

How did people travel in industrial Britain?

Transport experienced huge changes during the 18th and 19th centuries, which led to an increase in crime.

- ☑ The growth of the railways had a huge impact on society and crime.
- ☑ By the 1840s, railways had become a major form of travel.
- ☑ These were much faster than travelling by road and gradually became cheaper, so ordinary people could afford to use them.
- ☑ Crime on transport became a problem. Some railway companies hired their own police *(p.26)* forces to protect passengers.

How wealthy was industrial Britain?

Growing wealth led to more social change in 3 key ways:

- ☑ Two centuries of trade and industrial growth made Britain a wealthy country in this period.
- ☑ During the 19th century, the government collected higher taxes.
- ☑ They then used these to pay for reforms that would improve people's lives.

What was education like in industrial Britain?

4 key changes in education in the industrial period led to social change:

- ☑ In 1750, only a minority of children went to school.
- ☑ By 1880, the law *(p.26)* said all children up to the age of 13 had to attend school.
- ☑ By 1900, 95% of the population could read or write, compared with only 70% in 1850.
- ☑ This meant people could access more news and media, which had an effect on their attitudes to crime.

Were there protests in industrial Britain?

Revolutions around the world affected the British government's attitude to crime in 4 main ways:

- ☑ The American Revolution of 1775 caused the government some anxiety.
- ☑ The French Revolution at the end of the 18th century also rang warning bells for British MPs.
- ☑ They saw every protest or demonstration as the first sign of 'the British Revolution', and in the years after 1815 there was much protest.
- ☑ This affected the government's attitude to protest and crime.

What role did the government have in industrial Britain?

Over the industrial period, people's view of the role of the government changed in 3 key ways:

- ☑ For centuries, British people had resisted any government involvement in local affairs as an interference which threatened their freedom.
- ☑ However, by the 19th century, people began to accept the government should have some control over certain things.
- ☑ This meant they were more likely to accept a greater level of government control when it came to law and order.

What was the Enlightenment in industrial Britain?

During the industrial period, ideas about people's behaviour were changing in 2 key ways:

- ✅ During the 1700s there was a period known as the Enlightenment, when philosophers and thinkers argued about human nature.
- ✅ Some argued that improving people's education, along with their living and working conditions, might encourage better behaviour and less crime.

How did science affect crime in industrial Britain?

Changing ideas about science affected people's ideas about human behaviour in 2 key ways:

- ✅ In the mid-1800s, Charles Darwin developed his theory of evolution.
- ✅ This led some to believe that criminals came almost entirely from a class that was somehow less evolved than other people.

> ### DID YOU KNOW?
> ─────────────────────
> **Urbanisation has always led to more crime.**
> One reason for this is that towns and cities are more anonymous, unlike the countryside where everybody tends to know everyone else.

TRENDS IN CRIME DURING THE INDUSTRIAL PERIOD

Industrialised environments gave people new opportunities to break the law.

What was crime like in industrial Britain?

Rapid social and economic changes in Britain during the industrial period affected opportunities for crime and the types of crime that were committed. Overall, crime rates rose.

What types of crime were there in industrial Britain?

There were 4 key facts to note about changing patterns of criminal behaviour:

- ✅ Minor theft still accounted for 75% of recorded crime.
- ✅ Only 10% of crimes involved violence. Murders were rare.
- ✅ Key crimes from the early modern period *(p.34)*, such as witchcraft *(p.39)* and treason, declined.
- ✅ However, crimes against the person, property and authority all increased.

What new crimes were there in industrial Britain?

During the industrial period 3 key crimes became more prominent and caused more concern to society:

- ✅ Highway robbery *(p.55)*.
- ✅ Smuggling *(p.58)*.
- ✅ Poaching *(p.57)*.

What crimes declined in the industrial period in Britain?

By the 18th and 19th centuries 3 key crimes from the early modern period *(p.34)* declined:

- Cases of heresy *(p.41)* declined as the religious uncertainty of the Reformation had passed. The last execution for heresy took place in 1612.
- There were fewer cases of vagabondage *(p.38)*. As more people became wealthier, the fear of vagabonds greatly reduced.
- Cases of witchcraft *(p.39)* declined as more people became educated. They were less likely to believe such accusations, and in 1736 the witchcraft laws were finally repealed by King George II.

 ## What crimes against the person increased in 18th century industrial Britain?

The number of highwaymen increased. They attacked travellers, who were forced by threats or violence to hand over valuable possessions.

 ## What was the definition of smuggling as a crime in industrial Britain?

There were increasing numbers of smugglers in the industrial period. Smuggling *(p.58)* involved sneaking foreign goods into the country without paying the import duties (or taxes) on them.

 ## What kind of crime was poaching in industrial Britain?

Poachers committed property crimes by hunting illegally on private land. This had been mostly tolerated since Norman society and viewed as a 'social' crime, but it became a growing problem in the industrial period.

What kind of crime was garrotting in industrial Britain?

Garrotting involved partially strangling a victim so he or she could be easily robbed. There were several high-profile cases in 1861, and in 1862 an MP was garrotted near the House of Commons.

DID YOU KNOW?

People became increasingly concerned about crime in the 19th century.

Crime rose sharply between 1815 and 1825. This is believed to be the result of an economic slump after the Napoleonic Wars.

THE RISE AND FALL OF THE HIGHWAYMAN

Highwaymen were criminals on horseback who robbed and threatened travellers.

 ## What happened to highway robbery in the industrial period?

Highway robbery was an increasing problem during the industrial period, and became a serious concern to society. Some highwaymen became notorious.

 ## Why did highway robbery increase?

There were 6 main reasons highway robbery increased in the late 1600s and early 1700s:

- It had its beginnings in the chaos caused by the Civil War, but by the early 1700s it was more common.
- As trade increased there was more need to move goods and money around, so business people and ordinary travellers often carried large sums in cash.
- Turnpike trusts improved many road surfaces in the 18th century, charging travellers a toll to pay for the works. This meant more people travelling on the roads.

- While towns were growing, the countryside featured many isolated roads where robberies could take place.
- After wars ended, some demobilised soldiers struggled to find honest ways to make a living, and used their fighting skills as highway robbers instead.
- Highwaymen could hide and sell their stolen loot in taverns.

 ## Where there any famous highwaymen?

There are 2 key highwaymen who gained notoriety and fame for their exploits:

- One famous highway robber was Black Harry. He was eventually caught and executed.
- Perhaps the most famous highwayman was Dick Turpin. He gained a reputation as a heroic gentleman robber, but was accused of burglary, rape and violence before turning his hand to highway robbery. He was hanged in 1739.

 ## Why were highwaymen a concern?

The people and the government became increasingly concerned about highway robbery as the 18th century progressed due to 3 main reasons:

- Highway robbers were greatly feared by ordinary travellers because of their use of violence, threats, and sometimes murder.
- The authorities were concerned by the disruption to trade and the postal service.
- The worst areas for highway robbery were the major trade routes out of London.

Why did highway robbery decline?

There were 5 key developments that meant highway robbery declined just as quickly as it had grown:

- In 1772 the death penalty was introduced for anyone found armed and in disguise on a high road.
- Mounted patrols were set up around London. High rewards encouraged informers to report on the activities of highwaymen.
- The banking system became more effective over time and the number of banks increased. This meant there was less need for people to carry large sums in cash.
- Stagecoaches were introduced with regular staging posts where tired horses could be changed and travellers could rest for the night.
- Justices of the Peace refused to license taverns that were frequented by highwaymen.

DID YOU KNOW?

Highwaymen was the name given to robbers on horseback who attacked travellers.

Robbers who were on foot when they attacked travellers were known as 'footpads'. They worked in gangs and were similar to medieval outlaws who attacked people as they walked through the woods.

THE RISE AND FALL OF POACHING IN THE INDUSTRIAL PERIOD

As poaching laws tightened in the industrial period, more behaviours were classed as 'criminal'.

What happened to poaching in the industrial age?

Poaching, and the illegal hunting of animals, became increasingly common and was treated as a more serious crime in the industrial age.

What were the laws against poaching during the industrial period?

There were 3 key laws against poaching:

- ☑ The 1723 Black Act made hunting deer, hare or rabbits a capital crime. Anyone found armed, disguised, or with a blackened face in a hunting area could be prosecuted for poaching.
- ☑ Only landowners with land over the value of £100 a year could hunt. This was a huge sum and would have taken a labourer 10 years to earn. Anyone who owned land of less value, or rented land, was forbidden to hunt anywhere.
- ☑ Possessing dogs or snares that might be used for hunting was punishable by a £5 fine or 3 months in prison.

What caused the rise in poaching in the industrial period?

There were 4 main reasons why people poached:

- ☑ Most poachers were poor and some relied on poaching for food.
- ☑ A poacher might catch the odd rabbit or pheasant to supplement low wages.
- ☑ A minority of better-off poachers hunted for sport and entertainment.
- ☑ Many poachers would sell their haul on the black market and make large profits.

How did people react to harsh poaching laws in industrial Britain?

There were 3 main reactions to the harsh poaching laws:

- ☑ Many poachers formed poaching gangs who attacked gamekeepers.
- ☑ Villagers would provide an alibi for those accused of poaching.
- ☑ Many smaller landowners continued to hunt on their own land.

Why did poaching become less of a problem?

During the 19th century, the importance of poaching as a crime declined because of 3 main reasons:

- ☑ In 1823, the Black Act was repealed by Robert Peel.
- ☑ Poaching was still illegal but was no longer punishable by death.
- ☑ This caused a fall in social anxiety around poaching.

DID YOU KNOW?

It's believed the rise in poaching was a result of harsh new laws introduced in the industrial period.

Poaching laws made it illegal for small landowners to hunt on their own land.

THE RISE AND FALL OF SMUGGLING

Smugglers brought goods into the country by stealth to avoid paying import duties.

What happened to smuggling in the industrial period?

The number of people involved in the criminal activity of smuggling rose dramatically during the industrial period.

Why did smuggling increase in the industrial period?

There were 4 main reasons why there was a rise in smuggling:

- ☑ In the 17th century, the government introduced import duties (taxes) on a range of goods, like tea. This made them more expensive for people to buy.
- ☑ Smugglers brought goods into the country in secret, via the largely unguarded coastline. They could sell their goods more cheaply than traders who had to pay import duties, so they found a ready market and made a bigger profit.
- ☑ In the 18th century more goods - including cloth, wine and spirits - were taxed more heavily, and smuggling activity increased.
- ☑ Many people wanted to buy cheaper goods and viewed smuggling as a social crime, so they provided smugglers with a large and profitable market.

Why did smuggling become a more important crime?

There were 3 key different reactions to smuggling:

- ☑ At a time when there was no income tax and duties were the main source of government income, the authorities took smuggling very seriously.
- ☑ Ordinary people, though, usually turned a blind eye to smuggling. They were happy to pay lower prices for goods and disliked the expensive duties imposed by the government.
- ☑ People who lived near the large smuggling gangs, such as the Hawkhurst Gang in southeast England, were concerned about their lawlessness and violence.

Who became smugglers in the industrial age?

There are 5 key facts to note about people whom became involved in smuggling:

- ☑ Smuggling was profitable, and encouraged people from all walks of life into crime.
- ☑ In 1748, 103 people were officially 'wanted' for smuggling. Over 70% of them were labourers; fewer than 10% were small landowners; and the rest were tradesmen such as butchers and carpenters.
- ☑ Even wealthy people took part in smuggling, including government ministers!
- ☑ Some smugglers joined gangs, which could be as large as 50 to 100 men.
- ☑ They were well armed and would often use violence, so they had little fear of customs officers or the army.

Why did people become smugglers in the industrial period?

There were 5 main reasons why people got involved with smuggling:

- ☑ Smuggling gangs offered good pay. It was attractive to people because of the profits they could make.
- ☑ For farm labourers, smuggling was a quicker (and more exciting) way to make money than farming. A smuggler could earn 6 or 7 times a farmer's daily wage in a single night.
- ☑ Anyone who helped smugglers carry goods from ship to shore could expect to earn nearly twice a labourer's daily wage.
- ☑ The cloth, fishing and iron-making industries were similarly affected.
- ☑ Some wealthy people became 'venturers' and financed the ships that sailed to other countries to collect goods to smuggle.

Quizzes, amazing exam preparation tools and more at GCSEHistory.com

Why did smuggling decline?

Smuggling began to decline when it became less profitable because import duties were reduced. Non-smuggled goods were less expensive, so the demand for smuggled goods fell and smugglers made less profit.

DID YOU KNOW?

Smuggling gangs employed people to play a variety of roles.
For example, the 'spotsman' would guide the ships to shore, 'tubmen' were responsible for carrying the goods ashore, and the 'batsmen' protected them.

TRENDS IN PUNISHMENT DURING THE INDUSTRIAL AGE

As society changed during the industrial period, people began to question the effectiveness of deterrence in punishments.

 What form of punishments were there in the industrial period?

Between 1700 and 1900 punishments changed as the government began to focus less on retribution and deterrence, and more on reform.

 Which punishments were used less in the industrial period?

The use of 4 main punishments declined during the industrial age:

- ☑ The death penalty, after the end of the Bloody Code *(p.63)*.
- ☑ Public hangings after 1868.
- ☑ Corporal punishments, such as stocks and the pillory, were used less over the time period.
- ☑ Transportation ended in the 1860s.

 Which punishments were used more during the industrial period?

As some forms of punishment *(p.19)* declined in the industrial period, 2 other forms were relied on more and more.

- ☑ The use of prisons grew massively during this time.
- ☑ Although it was ended in the 1860s the use of transportation increased, especially at the end of the 18th and beginning of the 19th centuries.

 What were the punishment trends in the industrial period?

Changing ideas about society led to changing punishments during the industrial period in 4 ways:

- ☑ At the start of the 18th century punishments focused on deterrence, with a lot of painful and public punishment *(p.19)*.
- ☑ As time wore on, more people began to question their effectiveness.
- ☑ The authorities began to focus more on reform and less on deterrence.
- ☑ As a result, public execution and Bloody Code *(p.63)* declined, while prisons were put to greater use. Transportation was used more at first but ended in the 1860s.

 What happened to corporal punishment in industrial Britain?

The use of corporal punishment *(p.19)* declined during the 19th century in 3 main steps:

- ✅ Whipping was abolished for women in 1820.
- ✅ It was formally ended for men in the 1860s.
- ✅ It continued as a punishment *(p.19)* for offences in prison into the 20th century.

CHANGES TO TRIALS IN THE INDUSTRIAL PERIOD

Trials during the industrial period demonstrated continuity from early modern times.

❓ What were trials like in the industrial period?

There was little change in the trials system between the early modern period *(p.34)* and the 19th century. They did become longer, with lawyers for the prosecution and defence being introduced.

THE RISE AND FALL OF TRANSPORTATION

Transportation was a punishment that involved sending criminals far away to the mysterious lands of the New World.

❓ What was transportation?

Transportation was a punishment *(p.19)* that involved sending criminals overseas to faraway locations in the British Empire.

⚖️ What were the laws connected to early modern transportation?

Two important transportation laws were:

- ✅ The Transportation Act of 1718.
- ✅ The Transportation Act of 1769.

📍 Where were prisoner sent for transportation in the early modern period?

There were 3 main destinations where prisoner were sent for transportation in the early modern period *(p.34)*:

- ✅ At first, prisoners were transported to the British colonies in Maryland and Virginia in north America.

- ✅ Following the American Revolution in 1776, transportation to America stopped.
- ✅ Captain Cook discovered Australia in 1770, and in 1787 it was decided to send convicts there instead.

How many people were transported in the early modern period?

Transportation became an increasingly popular method of punishment *(p. 19)* during the 1700s.

- ✅ In total, 36,000 people were transported between 1718 and 1769.
- ✅ Between 1718 and 1769, 70% of prisoners convicted at the Old Bailey in London were transported.
- ✅ In total, historians estimate that between 50,000 and 80,000 prisoners were transported before 1770.
- ✅ 160,000 prisoners were transported to Australia between 1780 and 1860.

How long were transportation sentences usually for?

The length of a transportation sentence depended on the crime.

- ✅ Less serious crimes might mean a sentence of seven years.
- ✅ Those who were transported as an alternative to execution were often sentenced to fourteen years.
- ✅ Some criminals guilty of serious crimes were transported for life.
- ✅ However, even if they finished their sentence, transported prisoners were often unable to afford to travel back to Britain.

What were the benefits of transportation?

To the authorities in the 17th and 18th centuries, transportation seemed a good alternative to the death penalty for 5 main reasons:

- ✅ It was hard, dangerous and scary enough to be an effective deterrent.
- ✅ England did not yet have an effective prison system, so it was an alternative method of removal.
- ✅ Convicts could be used to populate and work on the new colonies that England wanted to establish in its empire.
- ✅ Transportation, unlike the death penalty, offered the opportunity for reform and rehabilitation.
- ✅ It took criminals away from the environments and habits that may have turned them criminal in the first place.

How did transportation develop in the industrial period?

Transportation to American colonies stopped in the 1770s, when America declared its independence. Australia, which had been claimed for Britain in 1770 by Captain James Cook, was chosen to receive 160,000 convicts from the 1780s to the 1860s.

Why did the use of transportation rise in the industrial period?

The use of transportation rose in the early industrial period for 6 main reasons:

- ✅ The discovery of Australia led to an increase in its use.
- ✅ It was hoped it would provide a punishment *(p. 19)* option less harsh than hanging, so juries would be more likely to convict.
- ✅ It was harsh enough to terrify people and deter them from committing crimes.
- ✅ It would reduce crime in Britain by removing those committing it.
- ✅ It would help claim the new land of Australia for Britain.
- ✅ It would reform criminals through hard work.

What was transportation like?

Transportation was a harsh punishment *(p. 19)* in 5 key ways:

- ✅ Following their trial, convicts were held in prison while they waited for the next ship to leave for Australia. As prison buildings were overcrowded, some were held in hulks - disused ships used as floating prisons just offshore. They worked in chains while they waited.
- ✅ On the transport ship to Australia, convicts were kept below deck in dirty, cramped conditions. About 1% died during the 3-4 month journey.
- ✅ On arrival, convicts were sent to work for settlers. Their new masters provided basic food and housing. Good conduct could bring early release.
- ✅ Prisoners who committed further crimes were flogged or sent to more distant settlements where treatment was frequently harsh.
- ✅ Prisoners who failed to complete their sentence and returned to Britain without a 'ticket of leave' proving early release were sentenced to death.

What was the impact of transportation?

When they had served their sentences, most convicts could not afford to return home so remained in Australia. Many took the opportunity to live peaceful lives, often becoming respected members of the community.

Why did transportation end?

Transportation to Australia eventually ended due to 5 main reasons:

- ✅ Transportation to Australia declined in the 1840s and officially ended in 1868.
- ✅ Settlers in Australia believed ex-convicts were responsible for keeping local wages down and crime levels in their towns high. They wanted to change the perception of Australia being a land of just criminals.
- ✅ The crime rate did not fall during the use of transportation - instead, it increased quite sharply.
- ✅ By the 1830s, it was costing half a million pounds every year. Prisons began to be used more frequently, partly because they were cheaper to run.
- ✅ Transportation came to be seen as more of an opportunity than a punishment *(p.19)* - wages were higher in Australia than in Britain, and gold was discovered there in 1851.

Who was sentenced to transportation?

There are 5 main facts to note about the prisoners transported in the industrial period:

- ✅ 80% of convicts sent to Australia were thieves.
- ✅ Most had committed more than one offence.
- ✅ Only 3% had been convicted of violent crimes.
- ✅ Some were people who had taken part in political protests.
- ✅ About a sixth of them were women.

DID YOU KNOW?

One reason for the decline of transportation was the growing expense.

By the 1850s, it cost £15 to keep a criminal in prison for a year, but £100 to transport them for 7 to 14 years.

THE USE OF HULKS

Hulks were old and mouldy warships used as an alternative to prisons.

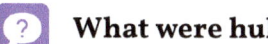 **What were hulks?**

Because of the lack of prison space, criminals sentenced to transportation often waited in makeshift prisons called 'hulks', made from disused warships.

What were the hulks like?

There are 6 main facts to note about experiences within the hulks:

- ☑ Living conditions on board hulks were usually very poor.
- ☑ The warships used for hulks were filthy and rotting, and disease was rife.
- ☑ Between 1776 and 1778, 25% of the prisoners in hulks died there.
- ☑ They were overcrowded.
- ☑ Prisoners worked in chains while they waited on the hulks.
- ☑ There were often riots and fights among the prisoners, which the jailers (or 'captains') could not always control.

When were hulks used?

Hulks were used between 1776 and 1787.

DID YOU KNOW?

Mortality rates on board the hulks were high.

Between 1776 and 1795, about 2,000 out of the 6,000 prisoners kept on the hulks died.

THE RISE AND FALL OF THE BLOODY CODE

The saying 'might as well be hanged for a sheep as a lamb' became popular during the Bloody Code.

What was the 'Bloody Code'?

The 'Bloody Code' was the name given to laws that made many more crimes punishable by death during the early modern period *(p.34)*. It marked a huge increase in the reliance on the death penalty as a punishment *(p.19)*.

When was the Bloody Code in use?

The Bloody Code lasted from 1688 to 1815.

How many laws were in the Bloody Code?

Between 1688 and 1815 the number of crimes that could be punished by death increased dramatically.

- ☑ In 1688, 50 crimes could be punished by death.
- ☑ In 1815, 225 crimes could be punished by death.

When did the Bloody Code end?

The Bloody Code was abolished in the 1820s when Robert Peel reformed criminal law *(p.26)*. Changing attitudes continued to push reforms throughout the 19th century.

 ## How did the Bloody Code end?

There were 7 main reasons for the ending of the Bloody Code:

- ☑ The reforms made to criminal law *(p.26)* by Robert Peel.
- ☑ Executions were meant to frighten people into obeying the law *(p.26)*, but instead they became cheap entertainment; the crowds laughed and drank while they were carried out.
- ☑ As crowds at public executions grew, the government felt it was becoming difficult to keep order. There was always the danger of escape or protest riots if the crowds had sympathy for the condemned criminal or felt the punishment *(p.19)* was unfair.
- ☑ Executions were not always carried out - even in the 1700s, only 40% of those sentenced to death were actually hanged. By the 1800s this had dropped to 10%. Criminals were often pardoned.
- ☑ Juries became more unwilling to convict people of minor capital crimes because they thought the punishment *(p.19)* unfair. This undermined the law *(p.26)* and might have encouraged some criminals to commit more crimes.
- ☑ Ideas about punishment *(p.19)* were changing. It was felt it should match the crime, and criminals could instead be reformed into thoughtful human beings.
- ☑ Transportation had emerged as the main alternative to capital punishment *(p.19)*.

 ## What was the impact of ending the Bloody Code?

There were 4 importan results of ending the Bloody Code.

- ☑ The end of the Bloody Code meant the use of harshly deterrent and retributive punishments fell.
- ☑ From the 1830s the only crimes punishable by death were murder and treason.
- ☑ Public executions ended in 1868.
- ☑ Transportation was abolished soon after.

DID YOU KNOW?

Hanging, drawing and quartering wasn't officially abolished until 1870.

The last person to be properly hanged, drawn and quartered was David Tyrie in Portsmouth in 1782. After this, although the sentence was used, it was only symbolic and the criminals were hanged until they were dead.

THE CASE OF THE TOLPUDDLE MARTYRS

The Tolpuddle Martyrs demonstrated how even small challenges to the status quo could lead to a harsh punishment.

 ## Who were the Tolpuddle Martyrs?

The Tolpuddle Martyrs were a group of farm labourers from the village of Tolpuddle in Dorset, led by George Loveless.

Quizzes, amazing exam preparation tools and more at GCSEHistory.com

What motivated the Tolpuddle Martyrs?

They were unhappy with their wages and working conditions, so tried to improve them by asking for an increase in their weekly pay. Their employers, the farm owners, refused - and then cut wages again.

What did the Tolpuddle Martyrs do?

The Tolpuddle Martyrs wanted to protect their wage levels so, in 1833, they formed a secret union. They swore an oath to keep it secret and support one another.

Why were the Tolpuddle Martyrs seen as a threat?

There were 4 main reasons the government saw the Tolpuddle Martyrs as a threat:

- ✅ The British government, genuinely afraid of rebellions and uprisings, was extra vigilant in looking for signs of conspiracy and plotting.
- ✅ The government feared the French Revolution of 1789 would inspire British people to do the same.
- ✅ The Swing Riots of 1830 saw 400 farm labourers destroy farming machines they blamed for keeping their wages low.
- ✅ The Grand National Consolidated Trades Union was set up in 1833. It aimed to bring all workers together, threatening business owners.

How were the Tolpuddle Martyrs caught?

They were caught when news of their secret oath was leaked to the rich landowners.

How were the Tolpuddle Martyrs tried?

Forming a union was not a crime so they were tried under old naval laws designed to prevent mutiny at sea.

How were the Tolpuddle Martyrs punished?

In 1834 Loveless and 5 other Tolpuddle Martyrs were sentenced to 7 years' transportation.

How did people react to the punishment of the Tolpuddle Martyrs?

The men were regarded as martyrs for union rights and a campaign was organised against their unfair treatment. One petition demanding their release was signed by 250,000 people. In 1836 the government granted all 6 men a pardon.

Why was the trial of the Tolpuddle Martyrs important?

The case of the Tolpuddle Martyrs shows how public opinion could influence what was regarded as a crime, and how the authorities punished people.

DID YOU KNOW?

The Tolpuddle Martyrs weren't told they had been pardoned while in Australia.

They only found out they were free to return to Britain when one of the men saw a newspaper report by chance.

THE END OF PUBLIC EXECUTION

Public executions, intended as a deterrent, were often treated more like a festival.

What were public executions in the industrial period?

They were a form of capital punishment *(p.19)* which regular citizens could attend. They were used to deter people from breaking the law *(p.26)* and defying authority.

When did public executions end in the industrial period?

The last public execution was in 1868.

What were public executions like in the industrial period?

Public executions in the industrial period had 4 important characteristics.

- ☑ By the 19th century, public executions had a festival atmosphere.
- ☑ They attracted huge crowds of people.
- ☑ They featured stalls, drinking and souvenir sales.
- ☑ They were seen as a form of entertainment, rather than a solemn and educational event.

Why did public executions end in the industrial period?

There were 6 key reasons why public executions ended:

- ☑ During the 19th century, the authorities became increasingly concerned about public executions.
- ☑ Factory owners resented having to give their workers the day off to attend executions.
- ☑ The crowds at executions might engage in drinking and prostitution, which could lead to further crime.
- ☑ The public viewed the executions as a party, rather than finding them a deterrent to committing crime.
- ☑ Several high-profile writers, including Charles Dickens, wrote scathing accounts of debauchery among the crowds.
- ☑ Large crowds were a possible threat to public order, especially if they sympathised with the criminal and disagreed with their sentence.

DID YOU KNOW?

Many people worried about the party-like atmosphere at public executions.

After he went to the execution of Maria Manning in 1849, Charles Dickens wrote about 'a sight so inconceivably awful as the wickedness and levity of the immense crowd collected at that execution'.

THE DEVELOPMENT OF THE USE OF PRISON

Prisons in the 18th century were organised haphazardly and had poor conditions.

What were prisons for?

Prisons were a minor form of punishment *(p.19)* until the 19th century, when their use was greatly increased.

How were prisons used in the 18th century?

There were 7 main ways prisons were used in the 18th century:

- ☑ During the 18th century and the early 1800s prisons were run along the same lines as previous centuries.
- ☑ Prisons continued to play only a minor part in the punishment *(p.19)* system.
- ☑ Prisons were run by towns and counties, with no national rules about their organisation.
- ☑ All prisoners were housed together - men, women, children, debtors, lunatics - regardless of the crime committed.
- ☑ Prison wardens were unpaid. They earned money by charging the inmates fees for their cell, food and clothing. They also charged them for their release or to see a doctor.
- ☑ The poor relied on local charities to pay their prison fees and lived in crowded, damp and dirty conditions.
- ☑ Richer inmates could afford their own room.

 ## How were prisons used in the 19th century?

During the 19th century there were 4 major reforms (changes) to the prison system:

- ☑ The government began a programme of major penal reforms (changes to the law *(p.26)* on punishment *(p.19)*).
- ☑ Imprisonment became the normal method of punishing criminals. By the 1860s over 90% of serious offenders were sent to prisons.
- ☑ The huge increase in the number of prisoners led to the government taking over the whole prison system and introducing regulations and inspections.
- ☑ Although it fluctuated across the 19th century, elements of rehabilitation were introduced to prison systems alongside the features that focused on retribution.

 ## Why did prison use increase in the 19th century?

There were 3 main reasons for government reform to prisons and the increasing use of them:

- ☑ The end of the Bloody Code *(p.63)* and concerns about transportation meant that by the mid-19th century, prison was viewed as a suitable alternative.
- ☑ The work of reformers John Howard and Elizabeth Fry influenced government thinking about how to run prisons. They wanted to see a greater focus on rehabilitation and reform.
- ☑ Fear of rising crime led to a demand for more effective punishments.

DID YOU KNOW?

Gaol fever killed many prisoners in the 1700s.
It was probably typhus, spread by lice.

THE IMPACT OF JOHN HOWARD ON PRISONS

A committed campaigner who lobbied to improve prison conditions.

 ## Who was John Howard?

John Howard lived from 1726 to 1790, and played an important role in prison reform.

Why did John Howard influence prisons?

As High Sheriff of Bedfordshire, John Howard was responsible for prisons in the county. He was shocked by the conditions that existed in them.

What reports did John Howard publish?

John Howard published The State of Prisons in England in 1777. This outlined problems in prisons of the time.

How did John Howard change the law?

John Howard successfully lobbied for 3 main changes to the law *(p.26)* on prisons:

- ☑ The Discharged Prisoners Act of 1774 abolished the practice of gaol fees. This was a payment prisoners had to make before they could be released, even if they had completed their sentence.
- ☑ The Health of Prisoners Act of 1774 made it law *(p.26)* that prisons should have bathrooms and sickrooms for prisoners.
- ☑ However, because prisons were run by local authorities, rather than the national government, these changes were not made across the country.

What did John Howard suggest?

In The State of Prisons in England, Howard suggested 3 key improvements for prisons:

- ☑ Better accommodation.
- ☑ Paid guards.
- ☑ Improved diets.

What impact did John Howard have?

Although Howard greatly influenced awareness and ideas about prison, national reform did not begin until after his death.

DID YOU KNOW?

John Howard devoted his life to improving prison conditions.
He died after catching gaol fever while investigating prison conditions in Russia.

THE IMPACT OF ELIZABETH FRY ON PRISONS

Horrified by what she witnessed, gentlewoman Elizabeth Fry campaigned for improved prison conditions.

Who was Elizabeth Fry?

Elizabeth Fry was an important reformer who influenced attitudes towards prison conditions.

Why was Elizabeth Fry concerned about prisons?

Brought up a Quaker, Elizabeth Fry had helped the homeless and was horrified when she saw conditions for female prisoners in Newgate Prison.

What actions did Elizabeth Fry take?

Elizabeth Fry worked to improve prisons in 3 main ways:

☑ She set up a society called the Association for the Improvement of Female Prisoners in Newgate Prison in 1817.

☑ She set up various education and bible classes for the female prisoners in Newgate.

☑ She campaigned tirelessly to change the law *(p. 26)* and conditions that prisoners experienced, and to raise awareness of the problem.

What impact did Elizabeth Fry have?

Elizabeth Fry helped bring about 4 key changes to prisons:

☑ She first made changes to Newgate prison, which were later introduced to other prisons.

☑ Clothing and furniture were provided for prisoners.

☑ Female wardens were provided for female prisoners.

☑ Schools were provided for women and children in prison, focusing on religious education.

DID YOU KNOW?

Elizabeth Fry was known as the 'Angel of Prisons'.
Her face was printed on the back of £5 notes between 2001 and 2017.

CASE STUDY: PENTONVILLE PRISON

With its famous panopticon design, Pentonville Prison was a ground-breaking experiment in new forms of punishment.

What was Pentonville Prison?

Between 1842 and 1877 the government built 90 new prisons in Britain. The first of these was Pentonville, which provided the model for the others.

What was the purpose of Pentonville Prison?

The building of Pentonville had 3 main purposes:

☑ It was built to deal with the increased number of serious criminals who were no longer being transported or executed for their crimes.

☑ It was set up not simply to deter; it aimed to reform the inmates.

☑ The changes to Pentonville prison represent the changes in attitudes to punishment *(p. 19)*.

How was Pentonville Prison designed?

Pentonville had an innovative new design.

☑ It had a central area with the 5 prison wings running out from it as spokes, so fewer guards were required to run the prison.

☑ Each wing was made up of dozens of individual cells.

☑ The prison also featured heating and a mechanical ventilation system.

☑ Altogether the prison could accommodate 520 prisoners.

What was the separate system in Pentonville Prison?

The separate system, tested in Pentonville, was intended to achieve 4 key things.

- ☑ Under this system, prisoners were kept apart as much as possible. They lived in separate cells and stayed there for up to 23 hours a day.
- ☑ It gave prisoners solitude to encourage reform through religious faith and self-reflection.
- ☑ It ensured prisoners were not influenced by other criminals who might encourage them to commit even worse crimes.
- ☑ The strength of the separate system was that it ended the fear prisons were acting as 'schools for crime'.

What were the problems with Pentonville Prison?

There were 2 key serious problems with the separate system in Pentonville Prison.

- ☑ It led to many prisoners going mad, having nervous breakdowns and even committing suicide.
- ☑ In addition, the system's requirement that inmates be housed in separate cells, made a separate prison extremely costly to build and maintain.

What were the cells of Pentonville Prison like?

The cells in Pentonville Prison were very small and had 4 key features:

- ☑ Each cell had a floor area of just 4 metres by 2 metres.
- ☑ There was a small, high window at the end to allow some natural daylight.
- ☑ The windows had thick glass and were fixed with iron bars for extra security.
- ☑ The cells also had piped water, a small basin for washing, and a basic toilet.

What were living conditions like in Pentonville Prison?

Living conditions in Pentonville were highly disciplined in 3 key ways:

- ☑ Prisoners were allowed out for a short period of exercise or to go to chapel.
- ☑ They had to wear face masks while exercising to stop them from speaking to each other.
- ☑ In chapel they sat in individual cubicles wearing masks made of brown sacking.

What kind of work did prisoners do in Pentonville Prison?

Pentonville prisoners had to engage in 6 main types of work:

- ☑ Some work in Pentonville was 'useful' work that would hopefully help prisoners find honest employment when they were released.
- ☑ Useful work included making clothes on a weaving loom in their cell.
- ☑ Some work, however, involved pointless tasks that were deliberately boring and repetitive.
- ☑ Pointless work included oakum picking, which involved unravelling and cleaning old rope.
- ☑ Prisoners might spend their time pointlessly walking a giant treadwheel.
- ☑ Prisoners might also have to turn a crank handle 10,000 times a day.

How did people view the work in Pentonville Prison?

Reformers believed useful work was better for prisoner rehabilitation. However, by the 1860s governments preferred prisoners to do pointless work because they believed it was more of a punishment *(p. 19)*.

How did the purpose of Pentonville Prison change?

The purpose of Pentonville Prison changed in 3 key ways:

- ✅ The 1860s saw attitudes to prison move from reform back to retribution. This harsher system continued for the next 30 years.
- ✅ Prisoners now faced more hard labour and minimum 5-year sentences for a second offence.
- ✅ Punishments became harsher.

What punishments were used at Pentonville Prison?

After the 1860s, punishments at Pentonville Prison became harsher in 4 key ways:

- ✅ Whipping.
- ✅ Electric shocks for those who didn't work hard enough.
- ✅ Bread and water diets.
- ✅ More time in solitary confinement.

Why did attitudes on punishment change in Pentonville Prison?

Attitudes to punishment *(p.19)* changed during this period in 3 main ways:

- ✅ People's fear of crime was increasing, even though the crime rate was falling. This was due to some highly publicised crimes, such as the Garrotting Crisis of the early 1860s, which the press blamed on the failure of the new reformed prison system.
- ✅ Critics said prisons were not reforming criminals but simply sending them back to the streets to commit more crimes.

DID YOU KNOW?

Before Pentonville, the first national penitentiary was Millbank Prison, opened in 1816 in Westminster, London.

It was a failure. It cost too much to run, the marshy land led to epidemics of disease, and the corridors were so complicated even the prison warders got lost.

THE DEVELOPMENT OF POLICING IN THE INDUSTRIAL PERIOD

During much of this period, policing was not seen as the government's responsibility.

What was policing like in industrial times?

In the early 18th century, the law *(p.26)* was still enforced using various methods employed previously. However, attempts at reform by individuals and the government in the 19th century saw more organised and effective policing.

How was policing in the industrial period the same as previously?

Policing in the industrial period remained the same as previously in 5 ways:

- ✅ Parish constables who dealt with disorderly behaviour, petty criminals and beggars.
- ✅ Watchmen, who were organised by parish constables and were responsible for protecting private property.
- ✅ Part-time soldiers who were used to dealing with rebellions or riots.
- ✅ Policing *(p.26)* mostly remained the responsibility of ordinary people in the local community.
- ✅ Some towns had salaried constables, watchmen and foot-patrols who were more experienced than part-time enforcement.

What were the problems with industrial period policing?

There were 5 main problems with policing *(p.26)* in the 18th century:

- ☑ Most law enforcement *(p.26)* officers were not paid. This made them less efficient as they did not have enough time or support, and also had full-time jobs.
- ☑ The few who were paid received low wages, and the job had low status.
- ☑ Some people were concerned that paid watchmen and constables had too close a relationship with the criminals they were supposed to police *(p.26)*.
- ☑ Urbanisation caused by mass migration from countryside to town made enforcing the law *(p.26)* more difficult. It was harder to keep track of people.
- ☑ Extreme poverty in some areas of big city areas, such as London, raised concerns about the growth of a criminal underclass.

How did policing change in industrial Britain?

The nature of policing *(p.26)* changed in 5 important ways:

- ☑ Some property owners and traders began to hire beadles to protect their premises from crime.
- ☑ To combat crime, victims might hire thief-takers to track down criminals and stolen goods.
- ☑ More gamekeepers were introduced to deal with the rise in poaching *(p.57)*.
- ☑ In 1748, the Fielding brothers set up the Bow Street Runners, a private policing *(p.26)* force that was professional and well-organised.
- ☑ Eventually, in 1829, the first uniformed government police *(p.26)* force was introduced in London. This system then spread around the country.

Why was there opposition to a police force during the industrial period?

By 1800, there were 3 main reasons people opposed the idea of a police *(p.26)* force:

- ☑ People thought it would be too expensive to fund.
- ☑ They thought it might be used by the government to limit freedom and privacy.
- ☑ They didn't think it would make a difference to law and order.

How did the government change policing in industrial Britain?

In the 18th century the government attempted to get involved in policing *(p.26)*, but it had limited success because of 2 main reasons:

- ☑ The government could not afford to increase the number of customs officers, which made them very ineffective.
- ☑ In Suffolk, in 1749 and in the 1780s, when the army put a temporary end to smuggling *(p.58)*, smugglers turned to highway robbery *(p.55)* and housebreaking.

DID YOU KNOW?

Government attempts at policing in the 1700s were not a success.

There weren't enough customs officials to stop smugglers. For example, in 1704, customs officials were outnumbered 200 to 8 when they disturbed a smuggling operation on the Welsh coast.

Quizzes, amazing exam preparation tools and more at GCSEHistory.com

THE BOW STREET RUNNERS

Originally known as 'Mr Fielding's People', the Bow Street Runners were an early prototype of the modern police.

What were the Bow Street Runners?

The Bow Street Runners were a team of thief-takers who patrolled the streets of London in the evenings. They also investigated crimes and gave evidence in court.

What did the Bow Street Runners do?

The Bow Street Runners helped combat crime in 6 key ways:

- ☑ They had regular horse and foot patrols in London, which were an effective deterrent.
- ☑ They investigated crimes.
- ☑ They presented evidence in court.
- ☑ They shared information about criminals with each other and with the public.
- ☑ They were more organised, professional and trustworthy than the thief-takers.
- ☑ Funded by a government grant, they introduced a horse patrol for 18 months that ended highway robbery *(p.55)*. When it stopped, however, the robbers returned.

How many Bow Street Runners were there?

The number of Bow Street Runners increased during the 1700s in 2 main ways:

- ☑ When the force was first set up, in 1748, there were 6 Bow Street Runners.
- ☑ By 1800, there were 68 Bow Street Runners.

What role did the Fielding brothers play in the Bow Street Runners?

Henry and John Fielding were brothers, and examples of individuals who improved policing *(p.26)*. After taking over at Bow Street Magistrates' Court in 1748, they realised more men were needed on London's streets to reduce crime.

What role did Henry Fielding play in the Bow Street Runners?

Henry Fielding played 3 main roles in the Bow Street Runners:

- ☑ Henry Fielding was the founder of the Bow Street Runners.
- ☑ He established a group of six men in 1748, known at first as 'Mr Fielding's People', to deal with crime in the area around Bow Street in London.
- ☑ He set up a newspaper called the Covent Street Journal to keep the public informed about crime and rewards.

What role did John Fielding play in the Bow Street Runners?

John Fielding had 4 important roles in the Bow Street Runners:

- ☑ In 1754 Henry Fielding's brother, John, took over the Bow Street Runners.
- ☑ He extended the force.
- ☑ In 1772 he launched a magazine called Hue and Cry, with information about crime and criminals.
- ☑ At first he charged fees for their services and collected rewards from the victims of crimes if successful convictions were secured.

How were the Bow Street Runners paid?

The method of payment for the Bow Street Runners changed in 3 key ways over time:

- ☑ At first, the Runners were paid one guinea a day by the Fielding brothers.

- ☑ They also took a share of the rewards offered by victims of crime.
- ☑ By 1785, the Runners were officially paid by the government and were the first modern detective force.

How did the Bow Street Runners share information?

There were 4 important ways the Bow Street Runners shared information:

- ☑ Because the Bow Street Runners talked to each other about criminals, Bow Street became a hub of crime intelligence.
- ☑ In 1752, Henry Fielding began to publish the Covent St Journal, with information about crime and rewards in the area.
- ☑ In 1772, John Fielding introduced The Quarterly Pursuit. This contained information about criminals, crime and stolen goods and was circulated to magistrates and the public, helping to create a national network of information.
- ☑ The Quarterly Pursuit later became known as Hue and Cry.

Why were the Bow Street Runners significant?

The Bow Street Runners, and the Fielding brothers' approach, was significant for 4 main reasons:

- ☑ The crime rate in Bow Street fell while conviction rates increased. This proved a paid policing *(p.26)* force was more effective than unpaid constables.
- ☑ The success of the Bow Street Runners led to more detective offices being set up in Middlesex and Westminster. In 1792, the Middlesex Justices Act set up further offices, each with 6 constables.
- ☑ The success of the Fielding's horse patrol led to a new patrol of 54 men being set up in 1805.
- ☑ Inspired by the Fieldings, the Thames River Police *(p.26)* was set up in 1798.

How were the Bow Street Runners limited?

The influence of the Bow Street Runners was limited in 2 key ways:

- ☑ The Bow Street Runners' work and influence was limited to parts of London - the old policing system *(p.26)* remained almost everywhere else.
- ☑ In addition, there was still no overall coordination between the different parts of law enforcement *(p.26)*.

THE METROPOLITAN POLICE FORCE

The first government-run police force was introduced in London in 1829.

What was the Metropolitan Police Force?

In 1829, the first government run, professional police *(p.26)* force was set up in London. It was known as the Metropolitan Police.

How was the Metropolitan Police Force set up at first?

The Metropolitan Police Force was set up in the following 4 ways:

- ☑ It was set up to combat crime in London.
- ☑ London was divided into 17 police *(p.26)* districts.
- ☑ The Metropolitan Police Force initially had 3,200 men.
- ☑ Each district was supposed to have 4 inspectors and 144 constables.

What was the Metropolitan Police Force Act?

The London Metropolitan Police Force was introduced by Home Secretary Robert Peel's Metropolitan Police Act of 1829.

What did the Metropolitan Police do when it first started?

When it first started, the Metropolitan Police had 4 main purposes:

- ☑ The focus of the new Metropolitan Police Force was to prevent, rather than solve crime.
- ☑ The emphasis for the new Metropolitan Police Force was on deterring criminals by having a public presence on the street.
- ☑ Constables patrolled their beats to counter crime.
- ☑ They also apprehended any criminals that were 'caught in the act'.

How did the Metropolitan Police develop in the 19th century?

The Metropolitan Police continued to develop in 5 key ways over the 19th century:

- ☑ In 1842 it set up the first detective force to gather evidence, investigate, and solve crimes after they had been committed.
- ☑ In 1870 police *(p.26)* helmets were introduced.
- ☑ In 1878 the Metropolitan Police detective force was reorganised into the Criminal Investigation Department (CID). This employed 200 detectives.
- ☑ A further 600 detectives were added to the CID in 1883. Over the next few years, this model was rolled out across the rest of the country.
- ☑ In 1883 a 'Special Irish Branch' was set up to monitor the activity of Irish terrorists called Fenians *(p.115)*. This later became known simply as Special Branch.

Who joined the Metropolitan Police?

Recruits to the London Metropolitan police had the following 3 main characteristics.

- ☑ Recruits were between 18 and 35 years old.
- ☑ Recruits were literate.
- ☑ Recruits were fit and healthy.

What problems did the Metropolitan Police have?

In the early days, the Metropolitan Police Force encountered some problems.

- ☑ The new police *(p.26)* force was not well-respected or popular.
- ☑ 2,200 police *(p.26)* officers were sacked for unprofessional behaviour in the first few years.
- ☑ Police *(p.26)* recruits were poorly paid, at one guinea for a seven-day week.
- ☑ It was considered a low-status job.

What was the purpose of the Metropolitan Police?

The Metropolitan Police had 4 important purposes:

- ☑ The role of the Metropolitan policeman was mainly to act as a deterrent.
- ☑ Constables patrolled the streets on a beat system to put people off committing crime.
- ☑ They wore a blue coat, to distinguish and disassociate them from the army, which wore red.
- ☑ They wore a tall, hard hat. This was partly to protect their head from attack, but also to stand on in order to look over high walls.

What was the London Metropolitan Police Force like in Victorian times?

The London Metropolitan Police in the late 19th century functioned in 5 ways.

- ☑ This was the first police *(p.26)* force set up by Robert Peel in 1829 and operated differently to other forces.
- ☑ The London Metropolitan Police policed the capital, including Whitechapel *(p.110)*.

- ☑ Unlike other police *(p.26)* forces at the time, the London Met was directly answerable to the Home Secretary in Westminster.
- ☑ In 1888, it had 13,319 police *(p.26)* officers for a population of about five million.
- ☑ This was about one police *(p.26)* officer for every 390 people, which wasn't seen as enough at the time.

What were the duties of the Metropolitan Police after 1870?

Officers had 8 key different duties:

- ☑ Dealing with accidents.
- ☑ Dealing with vagrants.
- ☑ Helping lost or homeless children.
- ☑ Dealing with lunatics.
- ☑ Dealing with problems in pubs.
- ☑ Dealing with problems with sewage.
- ☑ Dealing with traffic.
- ☑ Overall there were 82 laws relating to their role in the 1870s.

Who were the detectives in the years 1870 - 1900 in the London Metropolitan Police?

The detectives formed CID, about which there are 6 key points to note:

- ☑ CID stands for Criminal Investigation Department.
- ☑ It was first set up as a very small force in 1842.
- ☑ It was controversial. It wasn't clear whether it existed to prevent or solve crime, and people didn't like feeling they were being spied on.
- ☑ There was a corruption scandal in 1877, in which many detectives were found to have been taking bribes.
- ☑ Sir Howard Vincent was put in charge of setting up a new CID in 1878, which began as a force of 216 officers.
- ☑ Even after this, the CID was seen as quite corrupt. Its failure in the Jack the Ripper *(p.119)* case did not improve its image.

Who was in charge of the London Metropolitan Police during the Ripper case?

The Metropolitan Police was run by 5 key individuals during the Ripper case.

- ☑ The Metropolitan Police was answerable to the Home Secretary - in 1886, this was Henry Matthews.
- ☑ Edmund Henderson was Commissioner from 1869 to 1886.
- ☑ Charles Warren was Commissioner from 1886 to 1888.
- ☑ James Munro was Assistant Commissioner of the Met from 1884 to 1888, and then became Commissioner from 1888 to 1890.
- ☑ Howard Vincent was an influential Head of CID from 1878 to 1884.

DID YOU KNOW?

Early Metropolitan policemen had a reputation for unprofessionalism.

The first Metropolitan policeman was sacked after four hours for drinking on duty.

Quizzes, amazing exam preparation tools and more at GCSEHistory.com

THE DEVELOPMENT OF A NATIONAL POLICE FORCE

Following the establishment of the Metropolitan Police, forces were gradually set up across the country.

 How did policing change in the 19th century?

After the introduction of the Metropolitan Police Force *(p.74)* in 1829, Britain's central government gradually increased control of the setting up, organisation, control and funding of an official and professional police *(p.26)* force.

 Why did policing change in the 19th century?

Following the successful implementation of the London Metropolitan Police *(p.74)*, the government worked to spread the system across the country.

 How did the government change policing in the 19th century?

The government changed policing *(p.26)* through 3 main steps:

- ☑ In 1835 the Municipal Corporations Act allowed towns to set up their own police *(p.26)* forces.
- ☑ In 1839 the Rural Constabulary Act gave counties the power to set up police *(p.26)* forces. It also gave JPs *(p.37)* the power to appoint chief constables.
- ☑ In 1856, the Police *(p.26)* Act forced obliged all counties to set up a police force.

What problems were there with changes to policing in the 19th century?

There were 3 main limitations to the government's policing *(p.26)* reforms:

- ☑ To begin with, few Londoners had respect for the Metropolitan Police *(p.74)*.
- ☑ In 1835, the Municipal Corporations Act allowed towns to set up their own police *(p.26)* force. However, by 1837, only 93 out of 171 had done so.
- ☑ In 1839, the Rural Constabulary Act allowed counties to set up their own police *(p.26)* forces. By 1850, only 36 had done so.

Who paid for the changes to policing in the 19th century?

Financing changed in 3 main ways over time:

- ☑ At first, counties and towns were supposed to meet *(p.74)* most of the costs of their police *(p.26)* force, but over time the responsibility became more centralised.
- ☑ At first, the government was prepared to pay 25% of the costs from taxes.
- ☑ By 1876, the government was paying the half the running costs of police *(p.26)* forces that were run effectively.

When did the government change policing in the 1800s to make it compulsory across the country?

The government made it compulsory under the Police *(p.26)* Act of 1856 for all towns and counties to set up a police force.

Why did the government change policing in the 1800s to make it compulsory across the country?

There were 2 main reasons why the government changed policing *(p.26)* to make it compulsory:

- ☑ It had to be made compulsory because most areas of the country were slow to adopt police *(p.26)* forces.
- ☑ The law *(p.26)* also meant police forces would be inspected by government officials and only receive grants if their services were efficient.

What was the impact of the government making policing in the 1800s compulsory across the country?

By 1884 there were 39,000 police *(p.26)* officers in Britain and over 200 separate forces.

What technology was brought in by the police force during the 19th century to change policing?

Over the course of the 19th century, the police *(p.26)* force began to use 3 main types of technology to help it fight crime.

- ☑ From 1867, telegraph communications meant different police *(p.26)* stations and forces could communicate and share information quickly and effectively.
- ☑ In the 1880s they began to use photography to record crime scenes.
- ☑ Fingerprinting was first used successfully to secure a conviction in 1897.

 How much had policing changed by the end of the 19th century?

Towards the end of the 19th century, between 1870 and 1900, policing *(p.26)* had developed a great deal.

 Who joined the police after the government changes to policing in the 1800s?

In the late 1800s, police *(p.26)* recruits came from two main groups:

- ☑ About 31% came from the countryside surrounding their area.
- ☑ About 12% were ex-soldiers.

 What expectations were there about recruits after changes to policing in the Victorian era?

From the late 1800s, there were 3 main expectations of police *(p.26)* recruits:

- ☑ It was preferred if they came from the countryside, as people from the country were seen as stronger and more difficult to corrupt than townsfolk.
- ☑ They were expected to be well-disciplined, truthful, quick, energetic and able to keep control of their temper.
- ☑ They were expected to be literate - able to read and write.

 What were the benefits of joining the police after the government changed policing in the 1800s?

Those who joined the police *(p.26)* did so to gain 3 key benefits:

- ☑ A steady, if not high, wage.
- ☑ The possibility of promotion.
- ☑ After 1860, a pension if they served on the force for 30 years.

DID YOU KNOW?

Police uniforms changed over time.
In the 1860s policemen were encouraged to grow facial hair as it made them look fiercer and tougher.

INTRODUCTION OF NATIONAL CRIME RECORDS

National Crime Records allowed for better data and communication about crime.

 What were the National Crime Records?

The first National Crime Records stored information about crime and criminals for police *(p.26)* forces to access.

Quizzes, amazing exam preparation tools and more at GCSEHistory.com

When were the first National Crime Records set up?

They were set up in 1869.

CASE STUDY: ROBERT PEEL

Historians disagree over whether Robert Peel reformed law and order over matters of principle or pragmatism.

Who was Robert Peel?

Sir Robert Peel was an important British politician. As Home Secretary he introduced a wide range of changes to criminal law *(p.26)* and for reforming prisons, as well as the Metropolitan Police Force *(p.74)*.

What was Robert Peel's job?

Robert Peel played 2 important roles in government, from the point of view of crime and punishment.

- ✅ He was Prime Minister from 1834 to 1835, and again from 1841 to 1846.
- ✅ He was Home Secretary from 1822 to 1827, and again from 1828 to 1830. It was in this role that he introduced most of his crime and punishment reforms.

What were Robert Peel's strengths?

Robert Peel had 4 main strengths:

- ✅ He was well informed and open to new ideas. For example, after Elizabeth Fry spoke to Parliament about conditions in British prisons, Robert Peel took on board many of her suggestions in his work on penal reform.
- ✅ He was skilful at seeing bills through Parliament, carefully managing the reactions of other MPs. He used crime statistics to persuade fellow politicians to support his reforms.
- ✅ He made the most of his senior positions in government, as the home secretary and then prime minister, to implement his reform ideas.
- ✅ Some historians claim Robert Peel is the 'father of modern policing *(p.26)*'.

What helped Robert Peel set up the Metropolitan Police?

There were 5 other key factors that helped Robert Peel set up the Metropolitan Police *(p.74)*:

- ✅ Governments had become more involved in people's lives.
- ✅ The war with France (1803-1814) forced the government to raise more money through taxes. Local authorities were also given powers to raise their own taxes that could be used to pay for a police *(p.26)* force.
- ✅ There was widespread belief that crime, especially violent crime, was on the increase. The crime rate had risen sharply in the years following the French wars, when unemployment was a problem.
- ✅ After the French Revolution governments and landowners feared something similar might happen in Britain. High food prices and unemployment led to many large-scale protests after 1815, making a revolution seem likely.

☑ The rapid growth of towns had made the use of constables and watchmen seem inadequate, especially in London.

What were Robert Peel's views on punishment?

Influenced by reformers, Robert Peel advocated a system aimed at preventing crimes and reforming criminals, rather than focusing on punishments as a deterrent.

How did Robert Peel change the penal code?

Robert Peel reformed the penal code by reducing the number of crimes punishable by death by 100. Many minor crimes were punished more proportionately as a result.

What did Robert Peel do to prisons?

6 key changes were made to prisons.

☑ As Home Secretary, Robert Peel persuaded Parliament to pass the 1823 Gaols Act.

☑ Prisoners needed healthy conditions, with proper food, a fresh water supply and adequate drainage. They should be separated into groups so hardened criminals were not mixing with first-time offenders.

☑ Gaolers (those in charge of the jail) should be paid so they would not need to make money from prisoners. Magistrates had a duty to visit prisons and check on them.

☑ Male and female prisoners were to be separated. Female prisoners would be watched over by female warders.

☑ Prisoners were not to be held in chains or irons. In addition, they should attend chapel and receive religious instruction from the chaplains.

☑ Although the Act only applied to around 130 prisons and was ignored in some, it was an important step in improving conditions and aimed to reform the prisoners.

How effective were Robert Peel's reforms?

There were 2 main criticisms of the effectiveness of Robert Peel's reforms:

☑ His prison reforms had limited effect as there no paid inspectors to ensure the new laws were put into practice. There was no official prison inspectorate until the 1853 Prison Act was passed.

☑ Similarly, his police (p.26) reforms were mostly limited to London and it wasn't until after Peel's death in 1850 that all parts of the country had to adopt a police force as he envisioned.

What did Robert Peel do to policing?

Robert Peel introduced 2 important reforms to policing (p.26):

☑ He first took action on policing (p.26) in 1822 when he set up a day patrol of Bow Street Runners in London.

☑ By 1829 he had won support for the setting up of the Metropolitan Police (p.74).

What problems did Robert Peel's police force have?

Robert Peel's Metropolitan Police (p.74) faced 6 key criticisms:

☑ People had concerns this new police (p.26) force would be overly repressive, as in France, and would limit individual liberties.

☑ People worried the police (p.26) would be a military-style presence on the streets, not helped by many recruits being ex-soldiers or sailors.

☑ The police (p.26) were viewed as poorly trained and having immoral tendencies. Out of 2,800 constables in 1830, only 562 remained 4 years later.

☑ Drunkenness was a major problem, leading to 80% of dismissals.

☑ The police (p.26) weren't viewed as professionals. In 1836 in one force, 36% had previously been general labourers.

☑ Their pay of 21 shillings a week was less than a skilled worker earned. As a result, many constables would find alternative jobs.

How did Robert Peel try to solve the problems the Metropolitan Police faced?

Robert Peel is credited for overcoming many of the criticisms his Metropolitan Police *(p.74)* faced in 3 key ways:

- To ensure the police *(p.26)* force was viewed in a positive light, they had a uniform of blue overcoats and top hats to identify and distinguish them from the army.
- Any salary for the police *(p.26)* was an achievement considering this cost was the biggest cause of opposition to a police force.
- To combat views of the police *(p.26)* as violent, Peel had Metropolitan Police *(p.74)* commissioners draw up and issue clear guidelines to all new police recruits that emphasised the need to win over the public with respect.

How significant was Robert Peel?

It can be argued that Robert Peel was significant in 3 main ways:

- The principles of the Metropolitan Police *(p.74)* still provide the foundations for modern policing *(p.26)* in Britain today.
- The police *(p.26)* became accepted and respected. As first, they were called 'crushers' and 'raw lobsters'. By the 1850s they were more likely to be called 'Peelers' or 'Bobbies' - a reference to Robert Peel.
- While other factors were at play, crime rates fell steadily for 50 years from 1850 to 1900.

DID YOU KNOW?

Robert Peel died in 1851.
He was killed in a horse-riding accident.

TRENDS IN CRIME DURING THE MODERN PERIOD

The 20th century saw the growth of opportunities to commit new sorts of crime.

What is the modern period of crime and punishment?

Modern Britain is considered to be the period from around 1900 to the present. There have been more changes to crime and punishment during this time than any previous period.

What was the impact of war on modern attitudes to crime and punishment?

The 20th century witnessed two world wars (1914-1918 and 1939-1945) which changed attitudes to society, crime and punishment.

- The Holocaust influenced society to be more tolerant of minorities, and to question whether a government should be allowed to execute its citizens.
- The First and Second World Wars led to the public accepting a greater degree of control and interference in their lives.

How has growing wealth changed attitudes to modern crime and punishment?

By the end of the 20th century standards of living were better than in the early 1900s in 3 key ways:

- People lived in better houses, ate better food and, under the welfare state, government support like health care and unemployment relief provided protection for the most vulnerable members of society.
- However, the gap between the richest and poorest has continued to grow.
- The rise in both living standards and inequality has changed the nature of, and attitudes to, crime.

How has multiculturalism affected modern attitudes to crime?

The second half of the 20th century saw Britain become a more multicultural society in 4 main ways:

- ✅ In the 1950s, many people from Commonwealth countries (former British Empire colonies) moved to Britain to work.
- ✅ Britain joined what would later become the European Union in 1973 and enjoyed freedom of movement - the ability to travel, work and live without restrictions - across Europe.
- ✅ Over the next 50 years millions of Europeans would make Britain their home.
- ✅ This changed the makeup of society and raised issues around discrimination as a crime.

How has the changing position of women affected modern attitudes to crime?

During the 20th century, attitudes towards gender and crime changed in 4 key ways:

- ✅ In 19th century society, the common view was that men were the dominant partners in relationships. If they were violent towards their wives or partners, that was their personal business.
- ✅ The campaigns for women's votes at the beginning of the century led to some women gaining the vote in 1918, and all gaining the vote in 1928.
- ✅ Women's contribution to the First and Second World Wars enlarged their role in society.
- ✅ The 1960s campaigns for equal rights for women raised issues around inequality in the law *(p.26)*.

What are criminal trials like in the modern period?

Trials and courts saw 4 main important changes after 1971:

- ✅ The court system remained largely unchanged until the introduction of the Courts Act in 1971.
- ✅ This abolished the quarterly sessions and assizes.
- ✅ Now most criminal cases are heard in a magistrates' court.
- ✅ The most serious crimes are referred to Crown Court (which replaced visiting royal judges) and trials are heard before a jury.

DID YOU KNOW?

Newspapers have had a strong influence on the way people view crime.

The period beginning in the 1850s was known as the 'golden age of print' because taxes on newspapers were abolished and hundreds of new newspapers were introduced.

CRIME TRENDS IN THE 20TH CENTURY

Crime trends during the 20th century saw a continuous rise.

How did crime change in the 20th century?

The definitions of crime changed over the 20th century. Some past crimes continued in different forms and some new crimes were identified.

How much crime was there in the modern period?

There are 3 important factors to take into account when considering crime rates in 20th century Britain:

- ✅ The 20th century did see a rise in recorded crimes.

Quizzes, amazing exam preparation tools and more at GCSEHistory.com

- Some people argue the amount of crime committed isn't much higher than before - society is just better at recording it.
- Others argue that the percentage of those committing crimes has increased.

Why was more crime recorded in the 20th century?

The rise of crime in the 20th century can be attributed to people reporting it more frequently. There were 3 main reasons for this.

- The police *(p.26)* became more approachable, which led to violent crimes being reported more readily.
- The police *(p.26)* began to record crime consistently, which meant crime statistics appeared to increase.
- Additionally, the increasing use of technology, like telephones, made it easier to report crime. This made it appear that crime had risen.

Why did crime rise in the 20th century?

Various explanations have been given for the rise in crime during the 20th century, including these 10 possible causes:

- Unemployment.
- Inequality.
- Soft punishments.
- Materialism.
- Drugs.
- Poor access to education.
- Poor parenting.
- The media.
- Loss of discipline *(p.19)*.
- Loss of community.

What role did the media play to increase the fear of crime in the 20th century?

The media has played 3 key roles in increasing the fear of crime, separately from any rise in crime rates:

- Violent crimes receive widespread coverage.
- So do crimes where the victims are particularly vulnerable, such as the elderly or very young.
- These crimes make the headlines almost every day, so it seems as if we are living in the middle of a crime wave.

Who are the criminals in modern times?

There are 3 main sociological trends that are clear in the identity of 20th century criminals in Britain:

- At the end of the 20th century, 85% of recorded crimes were committed by men.
- Over half of these were committed by young men aged 21 and under.
- The crime rate among teenage boys increased faster throughout the century than for any other group.

What happened to the definition of crime in the 20th century?

Changing attitudes during the 20th century led to some behaviours being decriminalised, others becoming more criminal, and others being made illegal for the first time, thus creating new crimes.

Which behaviours are no longer crimes in the modern period?

Two main behaviours that were decriminalised during the 20th century were:

- Homosexuality *(p.85)*.
- Abortion.

Which behaviours became more criminal in the modern period?

Domestic violence *(p.88)* is an example of a behaviour that became more criminal as the 20th century progressed.

Which new crimes were there in the 20th century?

There were 5 main behaviours that became new crimes during the 20th century:

- ☑ Hate crime *(p.86)*.
- ☑ Race crime *(p.87)*.
- ☑ Driving offences.
- ☑ Consumption of some drugs.
- ☑ Conscientious objection.

What crimes continued in the modern period?

There are 9 types of older crimes that are still carried out in the 20th century but use different means:

- ☑ Theft.
- ☑ Terrorism.
- ☑ Social crimes.
- ☑ Murder.
- ☑ Smuggling *(p.58)*.
- ☑ Fraud *(p.92)*.
- ☑ Copyright *(p.90)* theft.
- ☑ Extortion *(p.90)*.
- ☑ Drug-taking.

How did theft change as a crime in the modern period?

Theft continued in the modern period in the form of shoplifting, which increased in the second half of the 20th century as more shops placed goods on display. This made shoplifting easier and more tempting. Car theft was also common.

What social crimes exist in the modern period?

There are both old social crimes that existed in previous periods and new social crimes in the modern period.

What old social crimes still exist in the modern period?

Some of today's social crimes are similar to those in previous periods, such as smuggling *(p.58)*, poaching *(p.57)* and copyright *(p.90)* theft.

What new social crimes were created in the modern period?

There are 3 main social crimes that are new:

- ☑ Tax evasion.
- ☑ Consumption of some illegal drugs.
- ☑ Minor driving offences.

What was murder as a crime like in the modern period?

Although the number of murders increased after 1900, the figures didn't rise as quickly as other crimes. The majority of murderers know their victim and have never committed a serious offence before.

How did smuggling change in the modern period as a crime?

Smuggling *(p.58)* changed in 4 main ways in the modern period:

☑ Improved transport during the 20th century has made smuggling *(p.58)* increasingly difficult to prevent.

☑ Legal *(p.26)* items such as drugs and tobacco might be smuggled to avoid import duties. This is known as social smuggling *(p.91)*.

☑ Illegal drugs might also be brought into the country. This is drug smuggling *(p.91)*.

☑ People might be brought into the country illegally, either to avoid immigration controls or to be forced into slavery. This is known as people smuggling *(p.91)* or human trafficking.

☑ Today, smuggling *(p.58)* of legal *(p.26)* items continues to be viewed as a social crime while the smuggling of people and illegal items is viewed as a dangerous crime.

DID YOU KNOW?

New wireless technology helped to catch Doctor Crippen in 1910.

After murdering his wife, he boarded a liner to Canada. Wireless technology was used to contact the Canadian authorities. Crippen was captured, returned to Britain and hanged.

THE DECRIMINALISATION OF HOMOSEXUALITY IN THE 20TH CENTURY

An end to homosexuality being against the law.

 What was the crime of homosexuality?

Male homosexuality - romantic or sexual attraction or behaviour between men - had been a crime since 1533. The Sexual Offences Act decriminalised male homosexuality for men aged over 21.

 When did homosexuality stop being a crime?

The Sexual Offences Act of 1967 legalised male homosexuality, although it was still illegal for men aged under 21.

DID YOU KNOW?

The last executions for homosexuality took place in 1835.

James Pratt and John Smith were hanged at Newgate.

HATE CRIME IN THE 20TH CENTURY

Prejudice and discrimination as a cause of crime has been viewed as increasingly serious in the modern age.

What is a hate crime?

Hate crimes are crimes committed specifically against a person because of a feature of their identity.

When were hate crimes criminalised?

In 2005 the Criminal Justice Act gave courts new powers to issue more severe sentences for hate crimes, including homophobic and racial attacks.

What makes a hate crime?

Two main behaviours define hate crimes:

- ☑ Homophobic crimes.
- ☑ Racial attacks.

How are modern hate crimes treated?

After 2005, if a person was attacked for being gay or because of their race, it would be classed as a hate crime and treated more seriously by the authorities.

DID YOU KNOW?

Hate crime continues to rise.

In 2014/15 there were 52,528 hate crimes reported. 82% of these were racially motivated.

THE DECRIMINALISATION OF ABORTION IN THE 20TH CENTURY

It was no longer illegal for a woman to terminate a pregnancy.

What was the crime of abortion?

Terminating a pregnancy was illegal in Britain and led to some women trying to end their pregnancies in unsafe ways.

When did abortion stop being a crime?

Abortion was decriminalised in 1967.

How was abortion decriminalised?

The 1967 Abortion Act legalised abortion provided certain conditions were met.

What were the conditions for the legalisation of abortion?

Legal *(p.26)* abortion was permitted as long as at least one of 3 conditions applied:

Quizzes, amazing exam preparation tools and more at GCSEHistory.com

- ☑ The child would be born with serious disabilities.
- ☑ The mother would be at risk of serious physical or mental harm if the pregnancy continued; this had to be independently agreed by two doctors.
- ☑ The pregnancy should not have progressed beyond 28 weeks.

DID YOU KNOW?

Before the legalisation of abortion, many women sought to end unwanted pregnancies illegally.

So-called 'backstreet abortions' were dangerous and could lead to long-term health problems or even death.

RACE CRIME IN THE 20TH CENTURY

Prejudice and discrimination were increasingly classed as criminal in the 20th century.

 What are race crimes?

As Britain became more multicultural, some new laws were needed to ensure that people from different minority groups were treated fairly.

 When did racial discrimination become a crime?

In 1968, the Race Relations Act made it illegal to refuse jobs, housing or public services to anyone on the basis of their race, ethnic background or country of origin.

 When did racial hate crime become illegal?

In the 21st century, laws against racial discrimination and attacks were strengthened in 2 main ways:

- ☑ In 2005 the Criminal Justice Act meant crimes based on racial hatred would result in harsher sentences.
- ☑ In 2006 a law *(p.26)* was passed to define the spreading of racial or religious hatred as a crime.

DID YOU KNOW?

The Race Relations Act of 1965 was the first legislation to address racial discrimination.

Before this, it was common for job applications to be rejected if the person had a 'foreign-sounding' name.

THE CRIMINALISATION OF DOMESTIC VIOLENCE IN THE 20TH CENTURY

The 20th century saw the introduction of harsher penalties for domestic violence.

 How was domestic violence criminalised?

During the 20th century, significant new laws were created to tackle violence and intimidation between people who were, or had been, in a relationship.

 What laws were passed against domestic violence?

During the 20th century, laws to protect people against domestic violence were strengthened in 3 main ways:

- ✅ The Domestic Violence Act, passed in 1976, gave victims the right to ask for an injunction against a violent partner. This meant a court would issue an order demanding the offender stay away from a person or place.
- ✅ In 1991, rape within marriage was recognised as a crime. It became possible to prosecute a husband for raping his wife.
- ✅ In 2014, the law *(p.26)* changed to make controlling and coercive behaviour towards a partner a crime. This could include telling a partner who they could see, what they could wear, or stopping their access to money.

DID YOU KNOW?

Current estimates say 1 in 3 women aged between 18 and 59 will experience domestic abuse in her lifetime.

DRIVING OFFENCES IN THE 20TH CENTURY

As technology advanced, definitions of crime changed to encompass the problems caused by careless driving.

 What are driving offences?

Driving offences is the term referring to a wide range of breaches of the laws governing road-users. Some, such as driving without an MOT, are considered relatively minor. Most others, such as driving while under the influence of drugs or alcohol, are viewed as serious in modern society. This is the result of government action.

 When did it become illegal to drink and drive?

Drinking and driving became illegal at the following 4 points in time:

- ✅ It was illegal to drive while under the influence of alcohol even before cars were even invented.
- ✅ Driving a horse-drawn coach while drunk first became illegal in 1872.
- ✅ It became illegal to drive a car while drunk in 1925.
- ✅ In 1967, a new law *(p.26)* set a maximum limit for the amount of alcohol a person could have in their bloodstream and still be legally fit to drive.

 When were driving laws passed about road safety in the modern period?

In 1935 all drivers had to pass a test, pay road tax, obtain insurance and maintain a roadworthy car. These rules came after many accidents - in 1934 alone, 7,343 people were killed on the roads.

Quizzes, amazing exam preparation tools and more at GCSEHistory.com

Why did drink-driving stop being a social crime?

Due to many people continuing to consider driving home after drinking large amount of alcohol as normal, the government began advertising campaigns highlighting the risks of drink-driving and the dangers of speeding.

How important are driving offences in the present day?

Today, driving offences absorb a huge amount of police *(p.26)* and court time. Car theft has become one of the largest categories of crime.

DID YOU KNOW?

The first fatal car accident in Britain occurred in 1899.

Two men were thrown from their vehicle in Harrow when the car's back wheel collapsed. Both died as a result.

DRUG CRIME IN THE 20TH CENTURY

Drug laws remained controversial throughout the 20th century.

What is drug crime?

The use of drugs has increasingly become a criminal offence as more substances have been made illegal.

What are the arguments for legalising drugs and stopping the use of them being a crime?

Many argue taking a drug should be a personal choice as long as it doesn't harm others, or that legalising certain drugs like marijuana would help in tackling other crimes such as gang-related violence.

When did drugs become a crime?

Many drugs first became illegal in 1971 when the Misuse of Drugs Act was passed.

How do the police deal with drug crime?

In the late 1970s drug squads were set up to stop the use and spread of illegal drugs. They raided buildings and disrupted the drugs trade, something that still happens today.

DID YOU KNOW?

In 1920s America, the prohibition of alcohol led to a massive rise in crime.

Gangs and organised criminals became rich and powerful by providing people with the alcohol they could no longer obtain legally.

EXTORTION IN THE 20TH CENTURY

The rise in technology has allowed criminals to find new methods of extortion in the modern age.

What is extortion?

Extortion involves obtaining something, usually money, through force, threats or blackmail.

How has extortion changed?

Methods of extortion have changed in 3 key ways in the modern period:

- ☑ In the past, it may have been carried out by using letters, the telephone or in person.
- ☑ Nowadays, the internet enables criminals to make threats on a wider scale.
- ☑ Some criminals extort money by threatening to hack businesses' computer systems unless they pay up.

DID YOU KNOW?

In 2017 the NHS was hit by a ransomware attack.

The attack affected key systems, forcing surgeries to turn away patients. Staff had to use pens and paper instead of computers.

COPYRIGHT THEFT IN THE 20TH CENTURY

The internet has made copyright theft an easier and more acceptable 'social crime'.

What is copyright crime?

Copyright is the right of an individual, collective or company to be recognised - and paid - as the owner (and often creator) of a work. Copyright theft is the use of works without the owner's permission.

How has copyright crime changed?

Copyright crime has changed in 4 key ways in the modern period:

- ☑ There are examples of this crime as far back as the 18th century, but the modern period has seen it increase due to modern technology.
- ☑ In the 20th century copyright theft could involve making a copy of a book, a cassette of music or a video recording of a film without paying the creator/owner.
- ☑ In the 21st century, copyright theft is committed when people illegally download music, computer games, films and television shows, or make copies of them. They sometimes then make them available to third parties.
- ☑ The internet makes it easier for people to access a huge selection of media more quickly than ever before.

DID YOU KNOW?

The maximum term for copyright infringement in 2020 is six months in prison or a £50,000 fine.

Quizzes, amazing exam preparation tools and more at GCSEHistory.com

SOCIAL SMUGGLING IN THE 20TH CENTURY

Smuggling goods to avoid import duties continued in the 20th century.

? What is social smuggling?

Tobacco and alcohol are smuggled into the country in huge quantities every day. Both are much cheaper overseas in countries where taxes on such goods are lower. Clearly there is big public demand for this.

> **DID YOU KNOW?**
>
> Tobacco smuggling still costs the British taxpayer about £2.2 billion a year.

DRUG SMUGGLING IN THE 20TH CENTURY

An increasingly serious problem in the modern age.

? What is drug smuggling?

Drugs are not the only illegal items smuggled into Britain, but they generate the biggest profits. Demand for illegal drugs has continued to rise over the modern period, particularly in the last 40 years. Consequently, the illegal drugs business has become a multi-billion pound industry.

> **DID YOU KNOW?**
>
> In 2016, two men were caught smuggling half a tonne of cannabis into Britain in a consignment of cheese.

PEOPLE SMUGGLING IN THE 20TH CENTURY

People smuggling is a growing problem in the modern age.

? What is people smuggling?

People smuggling is not a new crime. Slavery existed until 1833 and poor girls were sold into prostitution throughout the 19th century. However, people smuggling has increased in recent times and takes two main forms.

⚖ How does people smuggling involve immigrants?

Tougher immigration controls and conflict in different parts of the world have led to an increase in people smuggling. Immigrants who might otherwise not be allowed to enter Britain pay to be smuggled into the country.

⚖ How does people smuggling involve slavery?

Modern slavery involves people from poorer countries being brought to the UK and forced to work for very low or no wages. Some women and children are forced into prostitution and controlled by fear.

FRAUD

The rise in technology has increased opportunities to commit fraud.

? What is fraud?

Fraud is the use of deception for personal or financial gain. It generally involves impersonating other people or businesses.

How has fraud changed?

In the past this would be done by approaching an individual in person. Today, emails are used to trick people into revealing personal details such as bank or credit card information, or even persuading them to send money.

How is fraud handled?

Fraud is tackled by a specialist police *(p.26)* unit in 2 key ways:

- ☑ A national fraud squad was set up in 1946, with expert knowledge of finance, to tackle crimes in business and the stock market.

- ☑ It evolved to tackle other high-value crimes such as art theft, and is known today as the Specialist, Organised and Economic Crime Command.

TRENDS AND CHANGES TO MODERN POLICING

Modern policing in Britain has become increasingly comprehensive.

? What is policing like in the modern period?

Over the course of the 20th century, modern policing *(p.26)* saw some continuity but also many changes. It developed crime-fighting methods, improved the use of technology and became increasingly specialised.

What hasn't changed about the police in the modern period?

Policing *(p.26)* has remained the same since 1900 in 2 key ways:

- ☑ The powers of the police *(p.26)* to question, search, arrest or fine suspects, or report them to the courts, have changed little.

Quizzes, amazing exam preparation tools and more at GCSEHistory.com

☑ The police *(p.26)* are still overseen by the Home Secretary.

What problems did policing have at the start of the modern period?

By 1900, each area of Britain had its own local police *(p.26)* force, but there were still 7 key problems:

☑ Police *(p.26)* officers were badly paid and poorly trained. Training was similar to that of soldiers and featured military drills.

☑ Most of a police *(p.26)* officer's time was spent on the beat, walking around his local area and covering up to 20 miles per day.

☑ A policeman operated alone, on foot, with just a whistle to call for help and a wooden truncheon for protection. Pistols were kept for emergencies and locked up at the police *(p.26)* station.

☑ There were more than 200 local police *(p.26)* forces. Each had its own rules and ways of working, with little cooperation between the forces' 42,000 officers.

☑ Local record keeping was poor and there was no centralised system to store information about criminals. It was unusual and difficult for neighbouring forces to work together.

☑ Their main duties were dealing with petty theft and drunkenness, but their only crime detection tools were their eyes, ears and witness statements.

☑ All police *(p.26)* officers were male.

How has the police force changed in the modern period?

Over the 20th century and to the present day, the police *(p.26)* force has become broader and more representative in 3 key ways:

☑ In March 2015, the total number of officers was 126,818. These were spread across 43 local forces - down from about 200 - that worked together on many aspects of law enforcement *(p.26)*.

☑ Female officers first appeared in 1920. The proportion of female officers in England and Wales increased from 7% in 1977 to around 28% in 2015.

☑ The proportion of officers from ethnic minorities is still low, but has risen from 1% in 1989 to around 5.5% today.

What is police work like in the modern period?

The role of the police *(p.26)* has become wider and more varied in the modern period in 3 key ways:

☑ Police *(p.26)* officers deal increasingly with non-criminal incidents such as anti-social behaviour, drunkenness, missing persons and incidents linked to mental health where someone may be at risk.

☑ Officers also keep order at demonstrations, football matches and other large gatherings.

☑ As crime has become more varied and complex, many highly trained specialist departments and units have been developed.

What developments did policing have in the modern period?

The 20th century saw the introduction of 8 key new developments in policing *(p.26)*:

☑ Weapons.

☑ Transport.

☑ Crime detection.

☑ Training and recruitment.

☑ Communication.

☑ Duties.

☑ Record-keeping.

☑ Crime prevention *(p.26)*.

What weapons are used by police in the modern period?

The weapons used by the police *(p.26)* changed over time in 5 key ways:

- ✅ To distinguish them from soldiers, police *(p.26)* in 1900 were not armed.
- ✅ Nowadays, specialist police *(p.26)* can be issued with guns when necessary.
- ✅ Ordinary police *(p.26)* officers do not carry firearms but still have batons or truncheons.
- ✅ Pepper spray or CS gas can be used to control violent suspects.
- ✅ Some officers are trained in the use of tasers to temporarily disable a suspect.

How has police transport changed in the modern period?

Police *(p.26)* transport saw 3 main innovations in the 20th century:

- ✅ Since the 1930s, cars and motorbikes have improved police *(p.26)* response times. By the 1970s, these had effectively replaced the foot patrol or 'beat'.
- ✅ Police *(p.26)* helicopters track suspects and support officers on the ground.
- ✅ Today, many forces have reintroduced foot or bicycle patrols to build better community relations.

What new policing methods are there in the modern period?

There are 4 main new methods and technology for improving the detection of criminals that have developed over the 20th century:

- ✅ In 1901, the existence of blood groups was discovered, so chemical analysis of blood samples could help in detection.
- ✅ Also in 1901, the first national register of fingerprints was set up to help identify suspects.
- ✅ More recently, DNA samples have been used as evidence.
- ✅ Security video recordings and national TV programmes have helped in identifying criminals.

What is police training like in the modern period?

Since 1947, new recruits have undertaken 14 weeks of basic training at the National Police *(p.26)* Training College. Local forces have their own specialists to continue training.

How did police communication change in the 20th century?

Police *(p.26)* communication technology improved in the 20th century in 3 key ways:

- ✅ In the 1920s, Morse code transmitters were first installed in police *(p.26)* cars. Police telephone boxes were set up to provide a way to call for help.
- ✅ In the 1930s, two-way radios were introduced to police *(p.26)* cars and the 999 emergency telephone number was launched.
- ✅ Today, all officers carry a two-way radio for instant communication with their police *(p.26)* station or headquarters.

How has the police force grown in the modern period?

Over the 20th century, the police *(p.26)* force has developed 8 key units that specialise in a specific technology or crime:

- ✅ Dog units.
- ✅ Fraud *(p.92)* squad.
- ✅ Bomb squads.
- ✅ Drugs squads.
- ✅ National Hi-tech Crime Unit *(p.96)*.
- ✅ National Crime Agency *(p.97)*.
- ✅ Crime recording.
- ✅ Crime prevention *(p.26)*.

Quizzes, amazing exam preparation tools and more at GCSEHistory.com

How do police record crime in the modern period?

Since 1974, the police *(p.26)* national computer (PNC) has collected together several databases, including fingerprint, motor vehicles, and missing person details. Officers have access to national and local information 24 hours a day.

 How do police prevent crime in the modern period?

In the 2000s, police *(p.26)* focus has shifted more towards crime prevention in 7 key ways:

- In the 21st century, police *(p.26)* forces have increasingly focused on preventing crime by clamping down on factors that often lead to it.
- Every force appoints a crime prevention *(p.26)* officer (CPO), who advises local people on crime prevention and security.
- Police *(p.26)* community support officers are used to stop anti-social behaviour and reduce the fear of crime. They can confiscate alcohol and remove abandoned vehicles.
- They work with schools to educate young people about avoiding risks that can lead to them becoming victims of crime, and encourage them away from committing crime.
- They give people advice on making their homes more secure against burglary.
- They are involved with Neighbourhood Watch *(p.97)* schemes.
- They make risk and threat assessments - predicting where crime might occur, and profiling types of people who might be more likely to commit crime.

 How have police costs changed in the modern period?

Policing *(p.26)* changes during the modern period have added greatly to the cost of policing, which is now far higher than it was in 1900.

 Why has the police's reputation got worse in modern times?

The reputation of the police *(p.26)* was in decline by the 1980s due to 4 key reasons:

- Rising crime put police *(p.26)* work under the spotlight, and police methods were called into question.
- A series of scandals involving faked evidence, forced confessions and alleged racism eroded the reputation of the police *(p.26)*.
- The change of tactics to make the police *(p.26)* more technological meant the force also became more impersonal. Rapid-response teams in panda cars became a symbol of 1980s policing.
- On television, police *(p.26)* officers were often presented as tough and sometimes violent, likely to cut corners to meet *(p.74)* targets or get ahead.

DID YOU KNOW?

The annual police budget in 2018/19 was £12.3 billion.

THE INTRODUCTION OF DOG UNITS
The use of dogs to control and detect crime is a feature of modern policing.

 What are police dogs?

Police *(p.26)* dogs are trained to sniff out drugs, find explosives, track and catch criminals, and search for missing persons.

How has the use of police dogs changed?

The use of police *(p.26)* dogs increased in 3 main ways during the 20th century:

- ☑ From 1928, police *(p.26)* officers in south London used specially trained Labradors as police dogs on their beats.
- ☑ In 1946, a specialist dog section was established by the Metropolitan Police *(p.74)*.
- ☑ By the 1950s, most forces had dog units.

DID YOU KNOW?

The first police dogs in the UK were used in 1908 by British Transport Police at the docks in Hull.

There were four of them, named Jim, Mick, Vic and Ben.

THE INTRODUCTION OF BOMB SQUADS

A specialised team trained in the safe disposal of explosives.

What is the bomb squad?

The police *(p.26)* force has evolved to handle threats of terrorism and explosions with the introduction of bomb squads.

How were bomb squads developed?

The use of bomb squads has been developed in 2 key ways over the past 50 years.

- ☑ The Metropolitan Police *(p.74)* Bomb Squad and the national anti-terrorist squad were set up in 1971. There were an increasing number of terrorist attacks at this time, carried out by the IRA and others.
- ☑ Every police *(p.26)* force has its own Special Branch that works with MI5, the British security service, to detect and prevent terrorism.

DID YOU KNOW?

As well as modern threats, bomb squads often deal with explosive remnants of war, such as unexploded bombs from the Second World War.

THE NATIONAL HI-TECH CRIME UNIT

As technology increases the opportunities for crime, the police force has tried to keep pace.

What is the National Hi-Tech Crime Unit?

The National Hi-Tech Crime Unit, known as NHTCU, was set up in 2001 to tackle online crimes including hacking, credit card fraud *(p.92)* and virus attacks.

THE NATIONAL CRIME AGENCY

Leading the fight against organised crime.

What is the National Crime Agency?

The National Crime Agency (NCA), set up in 2013, is the lead agency against organised crime. This includes human, weapon and drug trafficking, cyber crime and economic crime, on both a national and international level.

THE NEIGHBOURHOOD WATCH SCHEME

Neighbourhood Watch schemes have handed some power of law enforcement back to local communities.

What is a Neighbourhood Watch?

Neighbourhood Watch is national network of local groups made up of volunteers. They raise awareness about crime and encourage neighbours to keep an eye on each others' property. Some estimates say 3.8 millions households are involved across the UK.

When did Neighbourhood Watch start?

The first Neighbourhood Watch scheme in the UK was set up in 1982, followed by thousands more.

Why did Neighbourhood Watch start?

There are 5 key reasons why Neighbourhood Watch was created:

- ✅ The reputation of the police *(p.26)* had declined by the 1980s.
- ✅ In his report on the Brixton riots of 1981, Lord Scarman said an important cause of the disturbances was that the police *(p.26)* had become out of touch with the community and had lost its support.
- ✅ Britain saw a dramatic rise in crime in the early 1980s and society was keen to see the introduction of new ways to tackle it.
- ✅ The idea of Neighbourhood Watch was imported from the US, where it was originally set up in Chicago and was seen to be successful in tackling crime.
- ✅ During the 1980s, Prime Minister Margaret Thatcher led a Conservative government that wanted to increase the roles and responsibilities of individuals and reduce the role of the state.

What were the aims of Neighbourhood Watch?

The 3 main aims of Neighbourhood Watch are:

- ✅ Helping the police *(p.26)* prevent crime by encouraging locals to be vigilant.
- ✅ Using community involvement to reduce fear of crime.
- ✅ Reporting crimes to the police *(p.26)*.

How effective was Neighbourhood Watch?

Some people believed the scheme made a significant and positive change. Others claimed it was ineffective and did not prevent crime *(p.26)*.

What were the strengths of Neighbourhood Watch?

Four of the main arguments made in support of Neighbourhood Watch schemes include:

- ✅ It works well for tackling issues like anti-social behaviour.
- ✅ It's very effective at making people feel safer and less vulnerable.
- ✅ The police *(p.26)* rely on local cooperation - they can't police effectively without community support.
- ✅ The scheme encourages local people to take an active part in making their community safer.

What criticisms were there of Neighbourhood Watch?

Three of the main criticisms of Neighbourhood Watch schemes include:

- ✅ Most Neighbourhood Watch groups are in wealthier areas that don't suffer from a lot of crime, rather than in those with high crime rates where they are needed.
- ✅ Neighbourhood Watch members are mostly older people who want an opportunity to be nosy neighbours and are unrepresentative of the whole community.
- ✅ The scheme is an excuse to underfund the police *(p.26)* service. It relies on unpaid volunteers doing jobs the police should be doing.

DID YOU KNOW?

Some six million households are believed to be part of Neighbourhood Watch.

THE USE OF TECHNOLOGY IN MODERN POLICING

Modern policing increasingly relies on technological advances.

⚙ How has science and technology affected policing?

Since 1900 new science and technology has enabled police *(p.26)* to work more quickly and to solve and prevent crime more effectively.

How has science and technology helped the police work faster?

Over time police *(p.26)* adopted technology in 4 main ways to improve their speed:

- ✅ In 1900, police *(p.26)* officers walked the beat and had a whistle to attract attention and call for help.
- ✅ In 1909, police *(p.26)* bicycles were introduced, allowing officers to pursue criminals more quickly.
- ✅ In the 1930s, police *(p.26)* cars were introduced to respond to crimes faster. Two-way radios were used to enable police officers to communicate with each other more easily.
- ✅ In addition, the 1930s saw the 999 emergency telephone number introduced to help the public contact the police *(p.26)* faster.

How has science and technology helped the police solve crime?

Since 1900, there have been 9 key advances in forensic science and technology have been adopted by the police *(p.26)* to help solve crimes:

- ✅ In 1901, a fingerprint branch was set up at the Metropolitan Police *(p.74)* headquarters at New Scotland Yard.
- ✅ Also in 1901, it was discovered there are different blood types.
- ✅ Improved microscopes made it possible to find smaller quantities of blood at crime scenes to use as evidence.
- ✅ In 1980, the Police *(p.26)* National Computer was launched, capable of holding the records of 25 million individuals.
- ✅ Improved DNA science led to the first murder conviction using DNA evidence in 1988.

Quizzes, amazing exam preparation tools and more at GCSEHistory.com

- ✅ In 1995, the National Automated Fingerprint Identification System and National DNA Database were set up to share information that could be used to identify criminals. By 2015 the DNA profiles of 5.7 million individuals were stored.
- ✅ More recently, CCTV has been used to identify and help convict suspects in criminal cases.
- ✅ Additionally, new software can rapidly analyse video data to identify criminals, such as the automatic number plate recognition technology that helps catch those committing driving offences. This would take far longer if a police *(p.26)* officer had to watch the video in real time.
- ✅ In 1900 photography was used to record crime scenes. Today improved communications technologies assist police *(p.26)* by recording and sharing information directly from a crime scene using tablets and smartphones.

How has science and technology helped the police prevent crime?

Technology has also been used by police *(p.26)* to prevent crime in 5 key ways:

- ✅ Breathalysers were introduced in 1967, enabling police *(p.26)* to test drivers' alcohol levels at the roadside. The invention made it possible to catch more drivers drink-driving and acted as a deterrent to others.
- ✅ Speed cameras were introduced in 1991, helping catch more drivers who were speeding and acting as a deterrent to others.
- ✅ Closed circuit television (CCTV) helps prevent crime *(p.26)*, as people are less likely to commit offences if they know they are being filmed.
- ✅ Computer software that enables mass video surveillance allows private companies to analyse large amounts of footage. It can help to forecast acts of terrorism and other crimes.
- ✅ Biometric screening uses unique physical characteristics, like fingerprints or eye patterns, to restrict access to data, places and buildings.

> **DID YOU KNOW?**
>
> The first speed camera in the UK was installed in 1991 on the M40 in West London.

DEVELOPMENTS IN PUNISHMENT IN THE MODERN PERIOD

Modern punishments have developed to offer many alternatives to traditional methods.

What were punishments like in the modern period?

The 20th century saw an end to most punishments of the past, notably capital punishment *(p.19)*. Authorities have continued to rely on fines and prisons, but the prison system has seen significant changes. Different governments have also tried non-custodial alternatives to prison, in particular for young offenders.

What happened to corporal punishment in the 20th century?

During the 20th century, there were 3 main steps in the move away from corporal punishment *(p.19)*.

- ✅ It was abolished as a punishment *(p.19)* for crime in 1948.
- ✅ It stopped being used in prisons in 1967.

> **DID YOU KNOW?**
>
> In 2016 it was estimated that 46% of all prisoners would reoffend within a year of release.

PRISONS IN THE MODERN PERIOD

Prisons have seen a gradual, but radical transformation from purely a punitive form of punishment to one that also embraces the concept of reforming the prisoner.

What were prisons like in the 20th century?

The 20th century saw significant changes to the way prisons operated and the inmates' living conditions. In the first half of the century there was support for the rehabilitation of offenders, as well as greater concern for the welfare of more vulnerable groups such as young people.

What happened to prisons in the 20th century?

Prior to 1947 there were 6 main changes to prisons:

- ✅ In 1896, Broadmoor Hospital was opened to house mentally ill prisoners.
- ✅ In 1902, hard labour on the crank and treadwheel was abandoned.
- ✅ In 1907, probation *(p.102)* was introduced. The person on probation had to report once a week to police *(p.26)* and meet *(p.74)* regularly with a probation officer. As long as they did not reoffend there would be no further punishment *(p.19)*.
- ✅ In 1922, solitary confinement was ended. Prisoners were allowed to talk with each other and were permitted more visitors. The standard uniform, which featured broad arrows, was replaced by ordinary clothes.
- ✅ From 1922 onwards, diet, heating and conditions in cells improved gradually. Teachers were employed in prisons to give inmates a better chance of finding work after release.
- ✅ In 1933, the first open prison was introduced at New Hall, Wakefield.

What were open prisons in the modern period?

There are 4 main features of open prisons:

- ✅ The rules at open prisons were more relaxed than those in traditional prisons of the time.
- ✅ Prisoners with minor records, those nearing the end of their sentence or those deemed not to be a threat were allowed to leave the prison to work for the day.
- ✅ This was to prepare them for ordinary life back in the community.
- ✅ The use of open prisons was expanded and continues today.

Why did prisons change before 1947 in the modern period?

There were 5 main factors resulting in changes to the prison system prior to 1947:

- ✅ Crime and fear of crime reduced, so there was less pressure on prisons to be seen to be harsh.
- ✅ Between 1910 and the 1930s, the prison population halved because more people were put on probation *(p.102)*. From 1914, people were given more time to pay fines.
- ✅ The belief that people inherited their criminal tendencies declined. Instead, many thought poverty or a criminal environment caused people to commit crimes. This raised hopes that better treatment and education in prison might reform inmates.
- ✅ There was a growing belief that the certainty of arrest rather than prison was the real deterrent.
- ✅ Prison commissioner Alexander Paterson was influential in pushing for and overseeing many changes to the prison system. He argued that probation *(p.102)* and rehabilitation were essential.

What happened to the prison population in the 20th century?

The prison population began to rise steeply after the 1940s. This trend has continued to the present day, with the number of of prisoners doubling to almost 90,000 between 1993 and 2015.

What caused the prison population to rise in the 20th century?

The rise in the prison population is due to several reasons.

Quizzes, amazing exam preparation tools and more at GCSEHistory.com

- ☑ Fear of crime increased after the mid-20th century and politicians reacted to public concerns that they were 'soft' on crime:
- ☑ The average length of sentences has increased. Prisoners are locked away for longer as governments seek to be 'tough on crime'.
- ☑ There is an increased chance of a prison sentence for certain crimes, particularly sexual, violent or drug-related offences.
- ☑ The number of people on remand (in prison as they await trial) has increased.

 ## What problems do prisons have today?

More recently, the prison system has had to deal with 5 key problems:

- ☑ Prison overcrowding peaked in the 1980s. Prisons have remained overcrowded since 1994.
- ☑ Reduced budget cuts and difficulties in recruiting have led to fewer staff looking after more prisoners.
- ☑ There have been ongoing problems with deaths in custody, which reached a record number in 2014.
- ☑ In recent years there has been a decline in purposeful activity such as work or education for prisoners. In 2014, Ofsted judged over half of prisons as inadequate or requiring improvement for learning and skills.
- ☑ The current cost of keeping someone in prison for a year is estimated at £40,000, and reoffending rates are high. Therefore, questions continue to be asked about the use of prisons as a punishment in modern society *(p.99)*.

 ## How did the government respond to the rise of the prison population in the 20th century?

In response to the growth in the prison population, coupled with underfunding, the government in the 1980s decided to build more prisons that were privately run. It also agreed on alternative punishments.

Why were the alternatives to prisons brought in the 20th century?

There were 3 main reasons why alternatives to prison were brought in:

- ☑ The pressures on the prison system.
- ☑ Changing attitudes in society that meant more people believed prisoners should have a chance to change rather than simply be punished.
- ☑ Modern courts often use alternative punishments that focus on reform and rehabilitation.

 ## What were the alternatives to prison in the 20th century?

There are 7 main alternatives to prison:

- ☑ Parole was introduced in 1967, allowing prisoners early release from prison if they behave well.
- ☑ Suspended sentences were also introduced in 1967. If offenders do not reoffend within a specified period of time, their sentence is waived.
- ☑ In 1972, community service orders were introduced. Criminals are required to do a number of hours work to benefit the community, such as clearing a rundown area or cleaning graffiti from buildings.
- ☑ In the 1990s electronic tagging experiments were introduced. These are a form of probation *(p.102)*. Offenders wear an electronic tag which lets police *(p.26)* observers know where they are at any time.
- ☑ In 1998, the anti-social behaviour order (ASBO) was introduced. This is a court order that places restrictions on what a person can do, for example where they are allowed to go or who they can talk to. They are usually issued to people who repeatedly behave in an anti-social way.
- ☑ Drug and alcohol treatment programmes offer support and treatment to people who got involved in crime because of their addictions.
- ☑ Restorative justice allows the criminal to meet *(p.74)* their victim to talk about what they have done and understand the impact it has had on others. In some cases, the meeting will be with a relative of the victim.

PROBATION

Probation is a modern punishment which offers an alternative to prison.

 What is probation in the 20th century?

Probation is a period of supervision. The offender is assigned a probation officer and has to follow certain rules.

THE TREATMENT OF YOUNG OFFENDERS IN THE MODERN PERIOD

The modern period has seen the introduction of a separate system for young criminals.

 How were young offenders treated?

The Victorian attitude to young offenders was harsh. They were viewed as juvenile delinquents and treated the same as adults. By the early 20th century, however, ideas were changing.

 How did the treatment of young offenders change?

By the 1900s, attitudes to juvenile crime were shifting away from harsh punishments and towards reform. Many believed that young people could be turned away from a life of crime through positive influences.

 What reforms were there for young offenders?

During the 20th century there were 6 key changes to the treatment of young offenders:

- ✅ The first borstal, located in Kent, was set up in 1902 for offenders aged under 18.
- ✅ In 1908, the Prevention of Crime Act created a national system of borstals. Those who designed the new system wanted borstals to emphasise education rather than punishment *(p.19)*.
- ✅ In 1932, the first approved schools were set up for offenders under the age of 15.
- ✅ The Criminal Justice Act of 1948 reduced the use of prison for juveniles and led to improvements in the probation *(p.102)* service for young people.
- ✅ The Children and Young Persons Acts of 1963 focused on the importance of caring for and protection for young offenders. It also raised the age of criminal responsibility from 8 years old to 10.
- ✅ The Children and Young Persons Acts of 1969 favoured supervision by probation *(p.102)* officers and social workers over prison sentences.

What were borstals for young offenders ?

There were 5 main features of borstals:

- ✅ Borstals were prisons for boys only, run rather like strict boarding schools, and existed from 1902 to 1982.
- ✅ The usual sentence was between 6 months and 2 years.
- ✅ Inmates could be released after 6 months if staff felt they were ready.
- ✅ Their purpose was to ensure young convicts were kept entirely separate from older criminals.
- ✅ Around 60% of those released went on to re-offend.

What were approved schools for young offenders?

There are main 3 facts to note about approved schools:

- ✅ Approved schools were rather like borstals and offered training in skills such as bricklaying.
- ✅ There was a great deal of public criticism of them in 1959, following riots and a large number of absconders.
- ✅ Approved schools were gradually closed as a result.

What did the Justice Act of 1948 do for young offenders?

There were 3 key reforms introduced by the 1948 Criminal Justice Act:

- ✅ A graduated system of prison, depending on the seriousness of the crime and the offender's record.
- ✅ Detention centres being introduced as a deterrent for young offenders, with a more relaxed regime than borstals.
- ✅ Attendance centres being used for young people aged 10-21 who had committed minor crimes. They attended daily or weekly compulsory sessions covering basic literacy and numeracy and life skills like money management and making job applications.

Why did reforms for young offenders decline?

In the 1980s, the system for young offenders was restructured in 2 key ways:

- ✅ As reoffending rates were still high and public opinion moved towards harsher punishments, several of the earlier reforms were abandoned.
- ✅ In 1982, the Criminal Justice Act abolished the borstal system and replaced borstals with youth detention centres.

What are youth detention centres for young offenders?

Youth detention centres represented a change in direction for young offenders' institutions in 3 main ways:

- ✅ Youth detention centres were introduced in 1982.
- ✅ They were intended to provide a short, sharp shock to young offenders by enforcing military drill and discipline *(p.19)*.
- ✅ However, this tougher stance failed to deter and re-offending rates continued to increase.

How are young offenders treated today?

There are 5 main punishment *(p.19)* methods currently available for young offenders:

- ✅ Parents being fined if they cannot keep their child under control, or having the child removed from parents and placed into care.
- ✅ Youth courts that work with agencies such as the police *(p.26)*, schools, social workers and probation *(p.102)* officers. The emphasis is on preventing the young person from settling into a life of crime.
- ✅ Custody is seen as a last resort. Offenders under 18 can be held in a secure children's home, a secure training centre, or a young offender institution. YOIs operate under many of the same rules as prisons.
- ✅ Attendance centres are the young offender's last chance. If they commit further offences they are locked up in a YOI.

☑ Non-custodial methods such as tagging and curfews are used to monitor offenders' movements, and courts can impose certain measures on youngsters, such as counselling.

DID YOU KNOW?

Borstals were so-called because the first one was established in Borstal, a village near Rochester, Kent.

THE ABOLITION OF CAPITAL PUNISHMENT

Capital punishment was decried as 'revolting and barbaric' by MP Sydney Silverman.

❓ What happened to capital punishment in the 20th century?

At the start of the 20th century, capital punishment *(p.19)* was still used - usually for the crime of murder. However, attitudes were changing and a range of laws were introduced that led to the abolition of the death penalty in the 1960s.

⚖️ How many people were executed in the modern period?

While public executions ended in 1868, after 1840 there were around 15 executions a year - all for murder.

⚖️ What were the arguments against capital punishment?

Abolitionists (those who wanted to end capital punishment *(p.19)*) began as a minority but had 4 main strong arguments:

☑ Other European countries had abolished capital punishment *(p.19)* without a noticeable increase in crime.

☑ Mistakes were made and sometimes the wrong person was executed.

☑ Most murderers acted on the spur of the moment and without thinking. Therefore, capital punishment *(p.19)* did not deter others from killing.

☑ Execution went against the teachings of different religions, and against the Christian ideals of forgiveness and the sanctity of life.

⚖️ What were the arguments for capital punishment?

Those who wanted to retain capital punishment *(p.19)* had 4 main arguments:

☑ It had a deterrent effect and criminals would be more likely to carry weapons if there was no danger of them being hanged for murder.

☑ Life imprisonment was expensive and, in a way, even more cruel.

☑ Murderers who served a sentence and were then released might kill again.

☑ Execution showed the proper contempt for murder and avenged the life of the victim.

⚖️ How did the Second World War impact capital punishment?

Following the Second World War and the horrors of the Holocaust, there was a growing feeling that execution was un-Christian and barbaric - an action one associated with Hitler's Germany rather than Great Britain.

⚖️ What about human rights and the death penalty?

There are 3 key points to note about human rights and the death penalty:

☑ The death penalty was challenged when, in 1948, the United Nations issued its Declaration of Human Rights, which Britain signed.

- ☑ It stated, 'Everyone has the right to life, liberty and security of person'.
- ☑ It also stated, 'No one shall be subjected to torture or to cruel, inhuman or degrading treatment or punishment *(p.19)*'.

 ## How did capital punishment decline in the 20th century?

Before the death penalty was fully abolished, 4 main steps were taken to limit the punishment *(p.19)*:

- ☑ In 1908, the Children's Act ended hanging of under-16s.
- ☑ In 1922, the Infanticide Act ended execution for mothers who killed newborn babies. This leniency was due to a better understanding of the impact of pregnancy and childbirth on the mental state.
- ☑ In 1933, hanging of under-18s was ended.
- ☑ In 1957, the Homicide Act limited the death sentence to 5 categories of murder - murder of a police *(p.26)* or prison officer; murder by shooting or explosion; murder while resisting arrest, while carrying out a theft; murder of more than one person.

What did Parliament do about capital punishment?

In Parliament, opinions about the death penalty were strongly divided. The House of Commons passed bills abolishing the death penalty in 1948 and 1956, but these were blocked by the House of Lords.

How did capital punishment end?

There are 4 important facts to note about the process of the abolition of the death penalty:

- ☑ In 1965, Home Secretary Roy Jenkins had strong views about ending the death penalty and his influence started the process of abolition.
- ☑ In 1965, the Murder Act suspended the death penalty for murder for 5 years.
- ☑ In 1969, an amendment to the Murder Act made the suspension permanent, except for a few crimes including espionage, arson in the royal docklands, and piracy with violence.
- ☑ In 1998, high treason and piracy with violence were no longer punishable by death.

When did opinions on the death penalty change?

In the 1950s, a series of 3 controversial executions caused the public to increasingly question the death penalty.

Why did opinions on the death penalty change?

There were 3 controversial executions that caused opinions to change:

- ☑ The execution of Timothy Evans in 1950.
- ☑ The execution of Derek Bentley in 1953.
- ☑ The execution of Ruth Ellis in 1955.

DID YOU KNOW?

The last execution in Britain took place in 1964.

Peter Allen and Gwynne Jones were executed for killing a van driver during a robbery.

THE CASE OF TIMOTHY EVANS, 1950

A sad demonstration of how the death penalty could lead to a permanent miscarriage of justice.

Who was Timothy Evans?

Timothy Evans was hanged in 1950 for murdering his wife and baby. Later evidence proved a serial killer was responsible for the murders and Evans was innocent.

THE CASE OF RUTH ELLIS, 1955

She was the last woman to be executed in Britain.

Who was Ruth Ellis?

Ruth Ellis was hanged for the murder of her violent and abusive boyfriend who had caused her to miscarry. She is famous because she was the last female to be executed in Britain.

When was Ruth Ellis executed?

Ruth Ellis was hanged in 1955.

Why was Ruth Ellis executed?

Ruth Ellis was hanged for murdering her boyfriend whom she shot.

Why were people against Ruth Ellis execution?

There were 3 main reasons why some people opposed her execution:

- ☑ The circumstances of the case. Ruth Ellis had suffered from physical abuse.
- ☑ She was also the mother of a young child who would be orphaned by her mother's execution.
- ☑ Some people were sympathetic and 50,000 people signed a petition against her death, but it was ignored.

DID YOU KNOW?

Ruth Ellis was a model, hostess and actress.

In 1951 she appeared in a film called 'Bikini Baby', although she was uncredited.

CASE STUDY: THE DEREK BENTLEY CASE

There was much debate over the meaning behind Derek Bentley's cry of 'Let him have it, Chris!'

Who was Derek Bentley?

Derek Bentley was a young man found guilty of murder and executed in 1953. His case was controversial and led the public to be more critical of capital punishment *(p.19)*.

Quizzes, amazing exam preparation tools and more at GCSEHistory.com

What did Derek Bentley do?

The 6 main events leading to Bentley's arrest in 1952 were well documented:

- [x] Bentley, along with his 16-year-old friend, Chris Craig, were caught burgling a warehouse in London. Craig was carrying a gun and he gave Bentley a sheath knife.
- [x] Detective Sergeant Fairfax climbed up and managed to arrest Bentley.
- [x] According to the police *(p.26)*, DS Fairfax asked Craig to hand over his gun, at which point Bentley shouted, 'Let him have it, Craig.'.
- [x] Craig fired at Fairfax, injuring him in the shoulder.
- [x] Bentley did not use the weapons in his pockets and made no attempt to escape.
- [x] More officers climbed onto the roof. PC Sidney Miles was immediately shot by Craig and killed.

What was Derek Bentley charged with?

Bentley and Craig were both charged with murder. Craig was too young to hang as he was aged under 18, but Bentley faced the death penalty if guilty.

What was Derek Bentley's trial like?

There are 3 important facts to note about the trial:

- [x] At the trial, Bentley and Craig denied Bentley ever said, 'Let him have it'.
- [x] Even if he had said it, Bentley's lawyer argued, he could have meant, 'Hand over the gun'.
- [x] There was also controversy over whether Bentley was fit to stand trial as he had the mental age of a ten-year-old child.

What was Derek Bentley's sentence?

Despite not firing the fatal shot, the jury found Bentley guilty. Although they recommended mercy, he was sentenced to death. Craig was imprisoned and not released until 1963.

How did Derek Bentley's lawyer react to his sentence?

Bentley's lawyers tried to appeal his sentence but were turned down.

How did people react to Derek Bentley's sentence?

There was a public outcry and 200 MPs signed a memorandum asking the Home Secretary, Sir David Maxwell Fyfe, to show mercy and cancel the execution.

When was Derek Bentley executed?

Despite pressure, Home Secretary Fyfe refused to halt the execution. Derek Bentley was hanged at Wandsworth Prison on 28th January, 1953.

How did people react to Derek Bentley's death?

There are 3 main facts to note about people's reaction to the execution of Derek Bentley:

- [x] 5,000 people protested outside the prison.
- [x] There were angry confrontations with police *(p.26)*. Some protesters ripped down and burned the death notice posted on the prison gates.
- [x] 2 people were arrested for causing damage to property.

How did Derek Bentley's family campaign for him?

There are 3 key facts to note about the campaign of Derek Bentley's family:

- ✅ Bentley's family campaigned for a posthumous (after death) pardon.
- ✅ They used the media to promote their cause and his case became widely known through songs, films and books.
- ✅ The campaign lasted more than 40 years.

When was Derek Bentley pardoned?

Derek Bentley was eventually pardoned in 1993. The murder conviction was quashed in 1998 by Court of Appeal.

How was Derek Bentley's execution significant?

The public outcry over the Bentley case contributed to the argument against the death penalty. Many believed it was a miscarriage of justice and made the law *(p.26)* look cruel. People doubted the morality of capital punishment *(p.19)*.

DID YOU KNOW?

Christopher Craig, who fired the shot that killed PC Sidney Miles in the Bentley case, was released from prison in 1963.

CASE STUDY: CONSCIENTIOUS OBJECTORS

Some people felt too strongly about war to participate - and were punished for their refusal.

What are conscientious objectors?

Conscientious objection, when people refused to take part in war for moral and/or religious reasons, became a new crime in the 20th century.

Why did it become a crime to conscientiously object?

As the First World War progressed, men lost the option to avoid the war.

- ✅ Up until 1916, everyone was free to have their own personal beliefs on war and violence.
- ✅ But in 1916 the Military Service Act was passed, which for the first time in the UK included conscription - compulsory military service for all unmarried men aged from 18 to 41. A couple of months later, it was extended to include married men.
- ✅ This made it illegal to avoid taking an active part in the First World War.

How did men become a conscientious objector?

There were 2 main steps to become a conscientious objector:

- ✅ The Military Service Act did allow for people refusing to join the armed forces on the grounds of conscience.
- ✅ Some 16,000 men made this request and had to appear before a special court called a tribunal which would judge their claim.

What were conscientious objectors' tribunals like?

There were 2 main reasons why the tribunals did not always give conscientious objectors a fair hearing:

Quizzes, amazing exam preparation tools and more at GCSEHistory.com

- ✅ The tribunals were held locally and the judging panel was selected by the local authority, so there was wide variation from area to area.
- ✅ Panel members were generally too old to be called up themselves but often had very clear views about other people's duty to fight and so were unsympathetic.

What alternative work could conscientious objectors be given?

There were 3 main outcomes from a tribunal:

- ✅ Non-fighting roles like driving ambulances at the front line.
- ✅ Supporting the war effort at home.
- ✅ However, some objectors were denied their request.

What happened to conscientious objectors when tribunals ruled against them?

Conscientious objectors were generally treated in one of two ways:

- ✅ Over 6,000 conscientious objectors were put in prison, where they faced solitary confinement, hard labour and a long sentence.
- ✅ Some were punished by being sent to France to the front line of the fighting. Once there they were given orders, they were sentenced by a military court if they refused to follow them. A small number were sentenced to death.

How were conscientious objectors affected by the harsh treatment?

By the end of the First World War, 73 conscientious objectors had died as a result of their treatment. Even after the war, all objectors were stripped of the right to vote until 1926.

What was the public attitude to conscientious objectors?

Public opinion of conscientious objectors was harsh and critical in 3 key ways:

- ✅ The majority of the public supported the war and were hostile towards conscientious objectors.
- ✅ They frequently accused them of cowardice, and some objectors were even physically attacked.
- ✅ Some objectors also received hate mail or white feathers in the post as a symbol of cowardice.

Why did the public have such a negative attitude towards conscientious objectors?

Objectors were treated harshly for 3 main reasons:

- ✅ The casualty rate of soldiers in the First World War was so high that the authorities were determined to stop pacifist ideas spreading. They feared it would hurt their ability to recruit soldiers.
- ✅ Refusing to fight was viewed as 'unmanly', and even traitorous and unpatriotic.
- ✅ Most people had close family and friends who were fighting and who had been killed or injured. They often felt objectors were unfairly shirking their responsibilities.

How were conscientious objectors treated during the Second World War?

During the Second World War, conscientious objectors were treated differently by the government in 3 main ways:

- ✅ Tribunals were still held but were no longer allowed to included ex-soldiers.
- ✅ A greater effort was made to give objectors alternative work such as farming or in industries like munitions.
- ✅ Prison was generally used as a last resort rather than a standard deterrent to other potential objectors.

Why were conscientious objectors treated differently during the Second World War?

Official attitudes to conscientious objectors changed in the Second World War because people were being asked to unite against Hitler as a tyrant and Nazism as a movement that persecuted minorities. In this context, harsh punishments for COs would have been seen as hypocritical.

How many conscientious objectors were there in the Second World War?

There were around 60,000 conscientious objectors in the Second World War.

DID YOU KNOW?

In the early years of the First World War, white feathers were often given to men who weren't in uniform as a way of showing they were seen as cowards.

THE AREA OF WHITECHAPEL

A maze of streets once described as 'a horrible black labyrinth'.

 What was Whitechapel?

Whitechapel is an area in the East End of London. At the end of the 19th century, it had a reputation for violence and crime.

 What was Whitechapel's history?

There are 2 main facts to note about the history of Whitechapel:

- ☑ In the 15th and 16th centuries, Whitechapel was quite a wealthy area.
- ☑ However, during the Industrial Revolution, industries sprang up there such as iron foundries, breweries and tanneries. These were quite noisy or smelly industries and made the area less pleasant to live in.

 What were conditions like in Whitechapel?

Living conditions in Whitechapel were notoriously poor and squalid. This was influenced by 8 key factors:

- ☑ Overcrowding.
- ☑ Housing.
- ☑ Industry.
- ☑ Streets.
- ☑ Lighting.
- ☑ Health.
- ☑ Sanitation.
- ☑ Pollution.

 Was it overcrowded in Whitechapel?

Whitechapel suffered serious overcrowding. Sometimes families of 10 or more would live in a one-bedroom house. In 1881, there were 188.6 people per acre in Whitechapel, compared to 45 people per acre in other areas of London.

 What was housing like in Whitechapel?

There were 3 main problems with housing in Whitechapel:

- ☑ The houses were often small and constructed from poor materials.
- ☑ They were poorly ventilated.
- ☑ There were a lot of 'rookeries' - areas of slum housing.

What sort of industries were there in Whitechapel?

There were 3 main types of industries in Whitechapel:

- ✅ Iron foundries, breweries and tanneries were smelly and caused pollution.
- ✅ There were a lot of 'sweated' industries, such as tailors, shoemakers and match factories, where people worked long hours in cramped, unhygienic conditions with poor ventilation for low pay.
- ✅ Slaughterhouses, butchers, bakers, the docks and railway construction often provided short-term low-paid work. This meant people weren't sure whether they would have a job from day to day.
- ✅ Many industries in the area were low paid. People might earn 6 to 12 shillings a week.

What were the streets like in Whitechapel?

Because of poor planning, Whitechapel had very narrow streets and alleyways, many of which ended in courtyards. It was described at the time as a 'labyrinth'.

What was lighting like in Whitechapel?

The thick smog and difficulty of lighting its narrow, maze-like streets meant lighting in Whitechapel was poor at night.

How was the health of the residents of Whitechapel?

Whitechapel residents suffered from poor health because of poverty and poor living conditions. In 1864 the death rate was twice as high as in other areas of London.

How was the sanitation in Whitechapel?

Sanitation in Whitechapel was poor in 3 key ways:

- ✅ Sewers often overflowed onto the streets.
- ✅ Clean water wasn't always readily available.
- ✅ The houses were poorly ventilated, which might lead to lung diseases.

What did the government do about living conditions in Whitechapel?

From the 1870s Whitechapel saw 3 key attempts to improve housing in the area:

- ✅ After the Artisans' and Labourers' Dwellings Act in 1875, the area around Flower and Dean Street was demolished.
- ✅ The residents of Flower and Dean Street merely moved to nearby Dorset Street and White's Row, where they still lived in poverty.
- ✅ In 1881 George Peabody opened the Peabody Estate, which comprised 286 flats with brick walls, better ventilation and shared bathrooms and kitchens. This represented much better affordable housing.

How bad was the pollution in Whitechapel?

Pollution and smoke from the factories in Whitechapel often mixed with the fog to form a dense, greenish smog that locals called a 'pea-souper'.

Why were people in Whitechapel so poor?

Whitechapel was infamous as a poverty-stricken area, partly because of the poor employment opportunities.

How were Whitechapel people employed?

There were 5 main forms of employment in Whitechapel:.

- ✅ Many tailors, shoe-makers and match factories ran sweated industries. Workers were crammed into small, badly-ventilated areas, sometimes working with harmful chemicals, for long hours.

- Wages were often low. Whitechapel residents generally earned 6 to 12 shillings a week.
- Many residents worked on the docks or built railways. This was short-term employment that often only offered a few days' work at a time.
- Whitechapel residents also worked in nearby butchers' and bakers' shops and abattoirs.
- Following an economic depression in the 1870s, many East Enders lost their jobs.

What were the workhouses like in Whitechapel?

There were 6 key features of workhouses in Whitechapel:

- These, such as South Grove Workhouse, were set up in the early 19th century to provide help and shelter, or 'relief', to the poor.
- They had deliberately unpleasant conditions to deter people from using them, so only the very poorest and most vulnerable went there.
- Workhouse residents were often unmarried mothers or the old, ill, orphaned or disabled.
- They were expected to do tough manual labour.
- Residents had to wear a uniform.
- Families were split up and could be punished for talking to each other.

What were the orphanages like in Whitechapel?

In 1870 Dr Barnardo opened an orphanage in the East End of London. By 1905, there were nearly 100 Barnardo homes, which offered kinder conditions than workhouses.

What did poverty studies of Whitechapel show?

There were 3 main findings of Charles Booth's poverty study:

- In 1891 Charles Booth's study found 37.5% of East End Londoners lived in dire poverty and couldn't afford to feed or clothe themselves properly.
- He produced a series of maps which showed Whitechapel had several 'vicious and semi-criminal' areas, such as Flower and Dean Street.
- His maps showed Whitechapel had great inequality, with some people living in comparative comfort and others in terrible poverty in quite close quarters to each other.

Why did people move to Whitechapel?

A lot of immigrants settled in Whitechapel, because many were poor and there was an availability of unskilled work and cheap housing.

Why were there Irish people in Whitechapel?

In the 19th century Whitechapel saw waves of immigrants coming from Ireland due to 3 main reasons:

- A lot of Irish people had moved to England in the 1840s because of the potato famine.
- Many Irish immigrants in Whitechapel were young men who came to London hoping to go on to America, but they lacked the boat fare and became stuck there.
- They got jobs as navvies, building the railways, road and canals. They also worked on the docks. These were very physically demanding, unhealthy and badly paid jobs.

Why didn't people like the Irish immigrants in Whitechapel?

There were 3 main reasons for the tension between the residents of Whitechapel and the Irish immigrants:

- Many Irish immigrants were young unmarried men. There was sometimes drunkenness and fighting, which led to negative opinions of them.

- ✅ Most Irish immigrants were Catholic. As such, they were seen as inferior by many Victorians and in some cases viewed as terrorists.
- ✅ Towards the end of the 19th century there was significant racial tension between the Irish and Jewish communities in Whitechapel.

Why were there Jewish people in Whitechapel?

There were 2 main reasons why Whitechapel saw a massive increase in the number of immigrants from eastern Europe, particularly Jews:

- ✅ In 1881, the assassination of the tsar in Russia led to 'pogroms' on Jewish communities in Russia.
- ✅ In the 1880s, 30,000 Jewish eastern Europeans fled to Britain.
- ✅ Many Jewish immigrants moved to Whitechapel, where they chose to be live en masse in certain areas. In some parts of Whitechapel, 95% of the population was Jewish.

Why didn't people like the Jewish immigrants in Whitechapel?

There were 6 main reasons why people did not like Jewish immigrants in Whitechapel:

- ✅ The high density of Jewish families in certain areas meant that they didn't mix much with the other Whitechapel residents and seemed separate and unfamiliar.
- ✅ Many Jewish immigrants were prepared to work for lower wages, and Whitechapel residents felt they were undercutting them.
- ✅ Some Jewish immigrants were sweatshop owners who were able to undercut other traders with their prices while treating workers badly.
- ✅ The Jewish Sabbath is on Saturday, so Jewish traders worked on Sundays. The Whitechapel traders felt this put unfair pressure on them to work on Sundays, too.
- ✅ The Jewish immigrants spoke a different language, ate different food and wore different clothes, which made them a more obvious target for hate or violence.
- ✅ Many eastern Europeans were associated with radical political ideas such as anarchism and socialism.

Why was there so much tension in Whitechapel?

Towards the end of the 19th century tensions in Whitechapel were escalating, with four groups or events proving significant.

- ✅ Irish nationalists (Fenians *(p.115)*) and other Irish workers protesting against unemployment and coercion in Ireland.
- ✅ Socialists.
- ✅ Anarchists.
- ✅ Poor workers who occasionally demonstrated.
- ✅ Bloody Sunday, where violence scarred a protest against the detrimental effects of English rule in Ireland.

Were there any demonstrations in Whitechapel?

There were an increasing number of strikes and demonstrations in London at this time and the police *(p.26)* did not always know how to react. The Bloody Sunday protest in 1887 is a famous example.

Why was crime so bad in Whitechapel?

Whitechapel had a reputation as a particularly criminal area, which was not surprising as there was extreme poverty, critical overcrowding, very poor housing and ethnic tensions. These elements ensured a high level of crime.

Was there a problem with drinking and drugs in Whitechapel?

There were 5 key reasons why drinking, alcoholism and drugs caused crime in Whitechapel:

- ✅ Many peoples' lives were hard and uncomfortable, and alcohol helped them forget that.

- Alcohol was cheap and widely available in Whitechapel.
- There were many pubs offering alcohol, but also warmth and food.
- There were several 'gin palaces' in Whitechapel. Their bright lights and big windows made them enticing.
- There were also a number of opium dens in Whitechapel.

Why did drinking cause crime in Whitechapel?

The popularity of alcohol and drinking in Whitechapel led to an increase in crime.

- It made people more volatile, reckless and prone to violence, so they were more likely to commit crimes.
- It made people less aware of their surroundings or able to protect themselves, so they were more likely to be victims of crime.

Why were prostitutes a problem in Whitechapel?

There were 7 main reasons why prostitutes caused problems:

- There were an estimated 1,200 prostitutes in Whitechapel in 1888.
- There were 62 brothels in Whitechapel when, in 1885, they were made illegal. This forced the prostitutes onto the streets.
- It was harder for women to find employment in Whitechapel.
- Alone on the streets at night, prostitutes were vulnerable to crimes such as theft, assault and rape.
- Prostitutes were at risk of unwanted pregnancies, and therefore also at risk from illegal backstreet abortionists.
- Despite the work of some campaigners at the time, the public tended to see prostitutes as immoral sinners.
- Prostitution itself wasn't illegal, but the police (p.26) often arrested prostitutes on other charges such as drunkenness.

What did the gangs do in Whitechapel?

There were a number of well-organised gangs in Whitechapel that had heavy involvement in crime in the area.

- They ran protection rackets, a scam in which gangs provide protection for a business for a regular fee and smash up the business if they aren't paid.
- They played a role in the illegal pubs and unlicensed boxing matches in the area.

How did people react to the Jews in Whitechapel?

There were 5 main reactions to Jewish people in Whitechapel:

- The arrival of large numbers of Jewish immigrants led to discrimination and a rise in criminal incidents against or involving them.
- Jewish immigrants were less likely to report crimes to the police (p.26) because they had suffered under the authorities in their countries of origin. There was also a language barrier as many did not speak fluent English.
- There were often attacks on, and crimes against, Jewish people, sometimes purely because they were Jewish.
- Some Christians preached to the Jews and tried to convert them, and this could lead to tensions and aggravation between large crowds of people.
- Protests against the long hours and low wages in Jewish-owned sweatshops could cause trouble for the police (p.26).

What was policing like in Whitechapel?

H Division, part of the London Metropolitan Police (p.74), was responsible for policing (p.26) in Whitechapel.

How did Whitechapel improve after the Jack the Ripper case?

Two laws were introduced by Parliament shortly after the Jack the Ripper (p.119) case that improved conditions in areas such as Whitechapel:

- In 1890, the Houses of the Working Classes Act was brought in to replace slums with low cost housing.

Quizzes, amazing exam preparation tools and more at GCSEHistory.com

✅ In 1890, the Public Health Amendment Act increased the powers of local authorities to improve sewers, pavements and rubbish collection.

DID YOU KNOW?

There were many doss-houses in Whitechapel where people could pay to sleep for a night.

Some offered a bench with a rope tied across it for tuppence a night. People could lean against the rope to sleep, and it was untied in the morning to wake them up.

FENIANS AND WHITECHAPEL

Fenians were outlawed Irish nationalists.

Who were the Fenians?

Irish immigrants were often associated with Fenianism and seen as terrorists.

What did the Fenians believe?

There was a political movement of Irish nationalism at the time and many Irish people wanted their own government and home rule. The extremist members of this movement were called Fenians.

What did the Fenians do?

In the second half of the 19th century the Fenians committed 2 key violent acts:

✅ In 1867, they blew up the wall of Clerkenwell Prison in London, killing several civilians.

✅ The 24th January, 1885, sometimes known as 'Dynamite Sunday' or the 'Fenian Dynamite Campaign', when the Fenians tried to blow up several London landmarks.

What were English attitudes to Fenians?

Many English people saw the Fenians as religious fanatics and terrorists, and they associated Irish immigrants with Fenianism. This caused tension and suspicion.

DID YOU KNOW?

The last man to be publicly executed in Britain was a Fenian.

Michael Barrett was hanged on 24th May, 1868, for his part in the Clerkenwell Prison explosion.

SOCIALISM AND WHITECHAPEL

Socialists were left-wing political activists.

? What is socialism?

Socialism was one of the new political ideas of the 19th century.

⚖ What do socialists believe?

Socialism is the belief that life and countries should be more equal. They often campaign for workers' and women's rights.

⧗ When were socialists active in Whitechapel?

Socialists were active in Whitechapel *(p.110)* between 1870 and 1900.

⚖ What was the influence of the socialists in Whitechapel?

There were 4 main ways in which socialists had influence in Whitechapel *(p.110)*:

- ☑ Some of the socialist groups in Whitechapel *(p.110)* were radical, believing in revolution and the overthrow of the government.
- ☑ The Social Democratic Federation was based in Whitechapel *(p.110)* and was involved in the 1887 Bloody Sunday demonstrations.
- ☑ The SDF was anti-police and, during campaigning for the London County Council elections, made a particular point of criticising police *(p.26)* shortcomings.
- ☑ The socialist newspaper, the Arbeter Fraint (the Workers' Friends) was printed in Whitechapel *(p.110)* by eastern Europeans.

⚖ How were socialists involved in Bloody Sunday in Trafalgar Square?

Bloody Sunday involved 7 main events:

- ☑ It was a protest involving many socialists that ended in a brutal police *(p.26)* response.
- ☑ At the time, there were numerous protests and demonstrations in Trafalgar Square which tied up police *(p.26)* resources.
- ☑ London Met Commissioner Charles Warren pressured the Home Secretary, Henry Matthews, to ban protests in Trafalgar Square.
- ☑ The response to this was a massive demonstration on 13th November, 1887. The police *(p.26)* response was seen as brutal.
- ☑ By the end of the day there were 2 people dead, 100 seriously injured, 45 arrests and 75 accusations of police *(p.26)* brutality.
- ☑ The demonstration led to a row that resulted in the sacking of Warren at the height of the Ripper investigation.
- ☑ The SDF was heavily involved and criticised the police *(p.26)* loudly following the event.

DID YOU KNOW?

The Socialist Democratic Federation was set up in 1881.

One of its members was George Lansbury, who became leader of the Labour Party. He was also the father of actress Angela Lansbury, the voice of Mrs Potts the teapot in Disney's Beauty and the Beast.

Quizzes, amazing exam preparation tools and more at GCSEHistory.com

ANARCHISM AND WHITECHAPEL

Anarchists were anti-government political activists.

(?) What is anarchism?

Anarchism was one of the new political ideas of the 19th century.

What do anarchists believe?

Anarchists hold anti-government, anti-authority beliefs.

When were anarchists active in Whitechapel?

Anarchists were active in Whitechapel *(p.110)* between 1870 and 1900.

What was the influence of anarchists in Whitechapel?

Anarchists were influential in 2 main ways:

- ☑ In 1871, anarchists managed to briefly overthrow the French authorities to establish the Paris Commune. When the authorities subsequently dismantled the commune, many of the leaders escaped to London - and Whitechapel *(p.110)*.

- ☑ The famous anarchist, Mikhail Bakunin, lived in Whitechapel *(p.110)*. He was under observation by Special Branch from 1893.

> **DID YOU KNOW?**
>
> The anarchist newspaper, Arbeter Fraint, was established in 1885 and printed in Yiddish, the Jewish language.

H DIVISION IN WHITECHAPEL

Part of the Met, H Division was responsible for Whitechapel.

(?) What was H Division?

H Division was the division of the London Metropolitan Police *(p.74)* responsible for Whitechapel *(p.110)*.

Who worked in H Division?

Records show that, at the time of the Ripper murders, H Division contained:

- ☑ 27 inspectors.
- ☑ 37 sergeants.
- ☑ 15 detectives.
- ☑ About 500 constables.

What did the H Division constables do?

There were 6 main roles that Constables of H Division fulfilled:

- ☑ They worked a beat system, patrolling an area in circles.
- ☑ During the day, one circuit of the beat involved about half an hour walking. At night, it would be 15 minutes.

- They would get to know the area well, and were expected to know the different buildings and businesses and talk to residents.
- They would have regular meetings with their beat sergeant and record their findings in a diary.
- They were monitored by the sergeant to ensure they were working their beat properly. They could be fined or sacked if they were considered to be slacking.
- It was a boring job with low pay, but policemen could expect to be promoted if they worked well.

Who were the H Division detectives?

There were 3 key H Division detectives:

- The lead detective on the Ripper case in H Division was Frederick Abberline. He had spent years policing *(p.26)* the streets of Whitechapel *(p.110)* before becoming an inspector.
- Inspector Edmund Reid spent 18 years as head of CID in H Division.
- Superintendent Thomas Arnold was an ex-soldier who joined the Met after leaving the army. He was chief inspector of H Division from 1874 before his promotion to head of the station.

What did the Whitechapel residents think of H Division?

The police *(p.26)* were unpopular in the Whitechapel *(p.110)* area for a number of reasons.

- There was a lot of poverty so people resented the government, which was represented by the police *(p.26)*.
- Crime was high, so people didn't feel well protected.
- There was a lot of alcoholism, prostitution and racial tension in Whitechapel *(p.110)*, so people resented the police *(p.26)* for interfering in their lives.

What was the role of H Division in Whitechapel?

The police *(p.26)* in Whitechapel *(p.110)* had 4 main roles in Whitechapel:

- Dealing with crime.
- Providing poor relief.
- Running soup kitchens.
- Looking after homeless and orphaned children.

Why was policing difficult for H Division?

Police *(p.26)* in Whitechapel *(p.110)* faced 4 key difficulties in dealing with crime.

- They were unpopular in the area, so people were less likely to give them information.
- The streets were very dark at nights.
- The streets were narrow and maze-like, which made it easier for criminals to get away.
- The area's social problems meant there was a lot of crime.

How did H Division improve after the Ripper investigation?

Following the Ripper case there were 3 key improvements in policing *(p.26)* in H Division:

- Record-keeping of known criminals, with the Bertillon system *(p.123)* and fingerprinting.
- Improved conditions in Whitechapel *(p.110)*.
- Communications between police *(p.26)* stations.

How did communication in H Division change?

Communications between police *(p.26)* and police stations didn't improve greatly in the years following the Ripper case. H Division had a telephone line installed in 1901 and bicycles for policemen in 1909, but this was much later than other police stations.

Quizzes, amazing exam preparation tools and more at GCSEHistory.com

Was there a reduction in crime in H Division after the Ripper case?

Crime increased after 1888 in 3 main ways:

- ☑ There was an increase in hooliganism, including young men deliberately frightening prostitutes by imitating the Ripper.
- ☑ There were more attacks on prostitutes. Prostitution continued and prostitutes remained vulnerable to crime.
- ☑ There was an increase in burglaries.

DID YOU KNOW?

Inspector Edmund Reid of H Division had an interesting hobby.

He was a keen hot-air balloonist.

JACK THE RIPPER

He terrorised Whitechapel, but his identity was never discovered.

Who was Jack the Ripper?

Jack the Ripper was a notorious and unidentified serial killer in Victorian Whitechapel *(p.110)*.

Was the Ripper's identity ever discovered?

One of the features of the Ripper case that continues to fascinate people is the identity of the killer, who was never discovered.

Who did Jack the Ripper kill?

Nobody is sure how many victims Jack the Ripper murdered, but historians are sure he was responsible for the deaths of five prostitutes, known as the 'Canonical Five'.

What did Jack the Ripper do?

Jack the Ripper murdered at least five women in the Whitechapel *(p.110)* area of London in 1888. He was never caught, but there were certain similarities evident in each case.

What did the crimes of Jack the Ripper have in common?

There were 3 main similarities between each of Jack the Ripper's victims, reflecting the killer's modus operandi.

- ☑ The victims were all prostitutes.
- ☑ They were all killed by having their throats cut.
- ☑ They suffered varying degrees of mutilation.

When were the crimes of Jack the Ripper committed?

The crimes of Jack the Ripper were committed between 31st August and 9th November in 1888. They stopped abruptly after the murder of Mary Kelly.

Who was Jack the Ripper's first victim?

The body of Mary Ann (Polly) Nichols was discovered on 31st August 1888. Her throat had been cut and her abdomen was cut open.

Who was Jack the Ripper's second victim?

Annie Chapman was murdered on 8th September 1888. It's thought she was probably strangled before her throat was cut and her intestines pulled out.

Who was Jack the Ripper's third victim?

There are 3 main facts to note about Jack the Ripper's 3rd victim:

- ☑ Elizabeth Stride was murdered on the night of 30th September, 1888.
- ☑ She was killed on the same night as the fourth victim, Catherine Eddowes.
- ☑ Her throat was cut but police *(p.26)* believed the killer was disturbed before she could be mutilated.

Who was Jack the Ripper's fourth victim?

Catherine Eddowes was murdered on the night of 30th September, shortly after the third victim, Elizabeth Stride. She was disembowelled and her face was mutilated.

Who was Jack the Ripper's fifth victim?

Mary Ann Kelly was killed on 9th November. She was eviscerated - most of her internal organs were removed, and her face was so badly mutilated it was unrecognisable.

Where did the Ripper murders take place?

Jack the Ripper's crimes were committed in and around London's Whitechapel *(p.110)* area.

- ☑ The body of Polly Nichols was found in Bucks' Row.
- ☑ Annie Chapman was found in George's Yard, just off Hanbury Street.
- ☑ Elizabeth Stride was found in Dutfield's Yard.
- ☑ Catherine Eddowes was discovered in Mitre Square in Aldgate. This was the only murder which came under the jurisdiction of the City Police *(p.26)*, rather than Whitechapel *(p.110)*.
- ☑ Mary Kelly was found in her rented room in Miller's Court.

How did the police try to find Jack the Ripper?

The police *(p.26)* used 8 main techniques to try to identify and catch Jack the Ripper.

- ☑ Post mortems and coroners' reports.
- ☑ Witness statements.
- ☑ Observations and sketches.
- ☑ Photography.
- ☑ Public information.
- ☑ Identity parades.
- ☑ Searches.
- ☑ Lures.

How did they use post mortems in the Ripper investigation?

There are 3 main facts to note about the use of post-mortems:

- ☑ The police *(p.26)* followed up information from coroners' reports and autopsies.

☑ After Annie Chapman's murder, the coroner believed the killer had 'considerable anatomical knowledge and skill'.

☑ The police *(p.26)* followed up by questioning doctors, surgeons, butchers and slaughterhouse workers.

How did they use witnesses in the Ripper case?

The police *(p.26)* used eyewitness accounts to investigate the crime. These were unreliable and often contradictory, but the police questioned around 2,000 people.

How did the police use crime scene observations in the Ripper case?

The police *(p.26)* carried out a number of observations when they discovered the bodies, writing down or sketching key features of the crime scenes.

How did the police use photography in the Ripper investigation?

Some photographs were taken of the bodies, both before and after the post mortem, and of the scene of the crime. This wasn't common practice, however, and it was probably the City of London police *(p.26)*, rather than H Division, that did so.

How did they ask for information from the public in the Ripper case?

After the double murder of Stride and Eddowes, the police *(p.26)* distributed 80,000 leaflets requesting information from people in the nearby area.

Where did the police search in the Ripper case?

The police *(p.26)* conducted searches of houses and buildings around the crime scenes.

How did they use identity parades in the Ripper case?

Identity parades were used to try to get witnesses to identify the killer. This was inconclusive, but they did manage to rule out some suspects.

How many extra police did they bring into Whitechapel during the Ripper case?

There are 2 main facts to note about extra policing *(p.26)*:

☑ 50 extra constables were sent to H Division, partly to help investigate the crime and partly to maintain law and order in a time of panic.

☑ The number of plain-clothes policemen had increased from 6 to 20 by October 1888.

What clues were there in the Ripper case?

There were 3 key clues in the Ripper case that the police *(p.26)* followed up to varying degrees.

☑ A bloody piece of Catherine Eddowes' apron was found under a graffito that read: "The Juwes are the men that will not be blamed for nothing". Sir Charles Warren had this graffito removed because of fears about anti-Semitic reprisals.

☑ Over 300 letters were written to newspapers and the police *(p.26)* from people claiming to be the Ripper. Although seen as hoaxes, some people believe a few may have genuinely been written by the killer.

☑ One of the letters was sent to George Lusk, the chairman of the Whitechapel *(p.110)* Vigilance Committee during the Ripper murders, along with half a kidney. The letter claimed the organ was from Catherine Eddowes' body.

Were there some techniques that weren't used in the Ripper investigation?

There were 5 key techniques that were not available to or were not used by the police *(p.26)* in the Ripper investigation:

☑ Fingerprinting wasn't in common use until the 1890s.

☑ They were unable to analyse blood.

- ☑ They considered using bloodhounds, and Sir Charles Warren did summon a pair of trained bloodhounds to be used at the crime scene. However, the police *(p.26)* did not make use of them.
- ☑ Although the formula for using body temperature to determine time of death had been developed in the 1860s, the victims' body temperatures were not scientifically measured.
- ☑ Identity sketches were developed by Bertillon, but weren't put into common use until the 1890s.

How successful was the Ripper investigation?

The Ripper investigation was a failure, both because it failed to identify and catch the killer, but also because it was badly criticised by the public and press.

What problems did the police face in the Ripper investigation?

H Division and the London Metropolitan Police *(p.74)* faced 5 main problems and impediments in identifying the killer:

- ☑ The media coverage.
- ☑ The crossover between H Division and the City of London police *(p.26)*.
- ☑ The lack of forensic evidence.
- ☑ The response of the public.
- ☑ The Vigilance Committee.

Why was the media a problem in the Ripper investigation?

There was a lot of competition between London newspapers, with 13 morning and 9 evening publications. They therefore competed fiercely to sensationalise the murders, creating a lot of misinformation as they did so.

What did the press do during the Ripper case?

The interference of the press caused 6 key problems for the police *(p.26)* investigation:

- ☑ They might add details to make their stories more interesting, basing a lot of their reporting on guesswork, rumours and untrustworthy interviews. Some of them added every murder in the area to the Ripper's tally.
- ☑ They criticised the police *(p.26)* heavily.
- ☑ They printed a lot of anti-Semitic accusations, such as making sketches of suspects look stereotypically Jewish. Sir Charles Warren ordered the graffiti near the Catherine Eddowes crime scene to be washed off due to the resulting tension.
- ☑ They created a lot of uncertainty and misinformation, and stirred up tension.
- ☑ They created a lot of false leads the police *(p.26)* then had to follow up, wasting time.
- ☑ They accused a man called Harold Pizer, or 'Leather Apron', of the murders, despite the fact he had an alibi.

Why were different police forces involved in the Ripper investigation?

Because Catherine Eddowes was killed in Aldgate, one problem faced in the Ripper investigation was that City of London Police *(p.26)*, who weren't part of the London Met, had to work alongside H Division, which was.

What forensics were there in the Ripper investigation?

The police *(p.26)* struggled to solve the Ripper case because of the lack of scientific techniques that were used to identify suspects later on. These including fingerprinting and blood analysis.

How did the public cause problems in the Ripper investigation?

The public response to the Ripper murders caused 4 key problems for the investigators.

- ☑ Over 300 hoax letters were written by people pretending to be the killer. This gave the police *(p.26)* more leads to follow up, which took time.
- ☑ Witness statements were contradictory and unreliable.

- ✅ The possibility of anti-Semitic reprisals meant the police *(p.26)* erased graffiti found near Catherine Eddowes' apron, which may have been a clue to the identify of the killer.
- ✅ The work of vigilantes, such as the Vigilance Committee, caused problems for the police *(p.26)* during their investigations.

How did the Vigilance Committee cause problems in the Ripper investigation?

The Vigilance Committee caused 3 main problems in the case of Jack the Ripper:

- ✅ They were a group of businessmen and traders from Whitechapel *(p.110)* who were frustrated by the lack of police *(p.26)* success and were annoyed about the lack of rewards offered for information, so they started their own reward system.
- ✅ They patrolled the streets with burning planks and made a lot of noise to deter the killer.
- ✅ The leader of the Vigilance Committee, George Lusk, was sent the 'From Hell' letter, along with half a kidney.

DID YOU KNOW?

It's believed Jack the Ripper was probably left-handed.

THE BERTILLON SYSTEM

A system of measurements to identify prisoners.

What was the Bertillon System?

The Bertillon System introduced the use of photographs and body measurements to record details of criminals.

When was Bertillon System introduced?

The Bertillon System was introduced in 1894.

Why was Bertillon System created?

The police *(p.26)* were criticised for having incomplete or non-existent records for known criminals, so the Bertillon System was introduced.

What replaced Bertillon System?

Eventually the Bertillon System was replaced by fingerprints. However, the Bertillon System of taking photographs of criminals remained.

COMMISSIONER EDMUND HENDERSON

He had a reputation as 'an easy-going chief'.

Who was Edmund Henderson?

Edmund Henderson was commissioner of the Met from 1869 until 1886.

What sort of person was Edmund Henderson?

There are 2 main facts to note about Edmund Henderson's character:

- ✅ Before becoming commissioner, Henderson had worked in Canada and in the penal colonies of Australia.
- ✅ He was known as 'an easy-going chief' because he didn't always sack policemen the first time they were found drunk on duty, and didn't mind if they grew beards.

What did Edmund Henderson do?

Edmund Henderson carried out 3 key actions as commissioner of the Metropolitan Police *(p.74)*:

- ✅ He set up a police *(p.26)* fund for the widows and orphans of policemen killed on duty.
- ✅ He arranged for policemen to get the vote.
- ✅ He set up a register of habitual criminals.

DID YOU KNOW?

Edmund Henderson was Comptroller-General of Convicts in Western Australia from 1850 to 1863.

COMMISSIONER CHARLES WARREN

He didn't serve for long, but was known as 'the man with the iron fist'.

Who was Charles Warren?

Sir Charles Warren had a short but eventful term as commissioner of the Metropolitan Police *(p.74)* from 1886 to 1888.

What sort of person was Charles Warren?

There are 4 main facts to note about Charles Warren:

- ✅ He was an army officer who served throughout the British Empire.
- ✅ He was reputed to be 'a man with an iron hand' when it came to running the police *(p.26)*.
- ✅ He was much stricter about discipline *(p.19)* than his predecessor Henderson, and increased the amount of drill in the force.
- ✅ He introduced more ex-soldiers into the force.

What events was Charles Warren involved in?

Charles Warren was involved in 2 main important events during his short time as commissioner:

- ✅ He was in charge of what became known as the 'London Dog Hunt', when policemen were told to seize dogs that weren't under proper control, to the disgust of the public.
- ✅ He was sacked at the height of the Ripper investigation after his response to criticism of his handling of the Trafalgar Square Bloody Sunday incident in November 1887, when two protesters were killed.

ASSISTANT COMMISSIONER JAMES MUNRO

At the start of the Ripper case, James Munro was second in command at the Met.

Who was James Munro?

James Munro was assistant commissioner of the London Met from 1884 to 1888, when he resigned. He was then made commissioner after Charles Warren was sacked at the height of the Ripper case.

HOME SECRETARY HENRY MATTHEWS

He was Britain's home secretary at when the Ripper first struck.

Who was Henry Matthews?

Henry Matthews became home secretary in 1886 and was in charge of the London Met at the time of the Jack the Ripper *(p.119)* investigation. He didn't get on with Charles Warren and sacked him in November 1888.

HEAD OF CID HOWARD VINCENT

A number of innovations were introduced under Howard Vincent.

Who was Howard Vincent?

Howard Vincent was a lawyer who was put in charge of the new Criminal Investigation Department in 1878.

What did Howard Vincent change?

Vincent made 4 key important changes to the CID.

- ☑ He wrote the first 'Police *(p.26)* Code' about the expected conduct of the police.
- ☑ He increased the pay for detectives to encourage better police *(p.26)* officers to apply.
- ☑ He increased the use of plain clothes in investigations.
- ☑ He centralised control of the detective force in the London Met.

DID YOU KNOW?

From 1883, Howard Vincent edited The Police Gazette.

A

Abolish, Abolished - to stop something, or get rid of it.

Abolition - the act of abolishing something, i.e. to stop or get rid of it.

Allegiance - loyalty to a person, group or cause.

Anarchism - the belief all government and organisation of society should be abolished.

Anti-Semitic - to be against, or hostile to, Jews.

Arson - the act of deliberately starting a fire.

Assassination - the act of murdering someone, usually an important person.

B

Beadle, Beadles - guards hired privately by shopkeepers and other businessmen to protect their premises from crime.

Bear-baiting - a blood sport which involves tormenting a captive bear, often by setting dogs to attack it.

Blood group - refers to the type of blood someone has and used to distinguish between different types for blood transfusions.

Bribe, Bribery, Bribes - to dishonestly persuade someone to do something for you in return for money or other inducements.

C

Campaign - a political movement to get something changed; in military terms, it refers to a series of operations to achieve a goal.

Captive, Captivity - to be held in prison or confinement.

Casualties - people who have been injured or killed, such as during a war, accident or catastrophe.

Catholic - a Christian who belongs to the Roman Catholic Church.

Civilian - a non-military person.

Claim - someone's assertion of their right to something - for example, a claim to the throne.

Clergy - those ordained for religious duties, especially in the Christian Church.

Collective responsibility - when a group of people is held responsible for an action or outcome, regardless of anyone's individual behaviour or performance.

Colonies, Colony - a country or area controlled by another country and occupied by settlers.

Commune - a place where a group of people live and work together and share resources.

Compurgation - part of the process of oath-taking in medieval courts.

Conscription - mandatory enlistment of people into a state service, usually the military.

Conservative - someone who dislikes change and prefers traditional values. It can also refer to a member of the Conservative Party.

Consolidate - to strengthen a position, often politically, by bringing several things together into a more effective whole.

Cooperate, Cooperation - to work together to achieve a common aim. Frequently used in relation to politics, economics or law.

Corrupt - when someone is willing to act dishonestly for their own personal gain.

Council - an advisory or administrative body set up to manage the affairs of a place or organisation. The Council of the League of Nations contained the organisation's most powerful members.

Counterfeiting - the act of producing a fake or fraudulent imitation of something.

Credit - the ability to borrow money, or use goods or services, on the understanding that it will be paid for later.

Customs taxes - a tax imposed by a government on products and goods coming into its country, making them more expensive.

D

DNA - the common name for deoxyribonucleic acid, a molecule that contains genetic information and instructions about the development, function and growth of every organism.

Decriminalisation, Decriminalise, Decriminalised - to make legal something that was previously illegal.

Demesne - land owned and retained under the direct control of a lord rather than leased out to a sub-tenant.

Deterrent - something that discourages an action or behaviour.

Discriminate, Discrimination - to treat a person or group of people differently and in an unfair way.

Dispute - a disagreement or argument; often used to describe conflict between different countries.

E

Economic - relating to the economy; also used when justifying something in terms of profitability.

Economic depression - a sustained downturn in the economy.

Electorate - a group of people who are eligible to vote.

Empire - a group of states or countries ruled over and controlled by a single monarch.

Estate, Estates - an extensive area of land, usually in the country and including a large house. It tends to be owned by one person, family or organisation.

Evolution - a theory by Charles Darwin suggesting human beings developed slowly from other animals, such as apes.

Excommunicate, Excommunication - to formally expel someone from the Catholic Church. Someone who is excommunicated is forbidden from participating in sacraments and services, and often believes their soul is condemned.

Extreme - furthest from the centre or any given point. If someone holds extreme views, they are not moderate and are considered radical.

F

Famine - a severe food shortage resulting in starvation and death, usually the result of bad harvests.

Fasting - to deliberately refrain from eating, and often drinking, for a period of time.

Front - in war, the area where fighting is taking place.

Fyrd - an army that could be raised by the king if needed to fight in Anglo-Saxon England. Every five hides had to provide a man to fight in the fyrd for a maximum of 40 days.

G

Gamekeeper, Gamekeepers - someone employed to manage an area of land, such as an estate or woodland. They will usually breed game and protect it from poachers and predators.

H

Harvest - the process of gathering and collecting crops.

Hide - a measurement of land in Saxon times, equivalent to around 120 acres.

I

Idle - to be lazy and avoid work, having no purpose and preferring to do nothing.

Illiterate - unable to read or write.

Immigrant - someone who moves to another country.

Immigration - the act of coming to a foreign country with the intention of living there permanently.

Import - to bring goods or services into a different country to sell.

Import duty, Import tariffs - a tax imposed by a government on products and goods coming into its country, making them more expensive.

Independence, Independent - to be free of control, often meaning by another country, allowing the people of a nation the ability to govern themselves.

Industrial - related to industry, manufacturing and/or production.

Industry - the part of the economy concerned with turning raw materials into into manufactured goods, for example making furniture from wood.

Inferior - lower in rank, status or quality.

Innovate, Innovation - the introduction and development of new things, such as inventions, methods or ideas.

J

Juries, Jury - a group of people sworn to listen to evidence on a legal case and then deliver an impartial verdict based on what they have heard.

L

Legitimacy, Legitimate - accepted by law or conforming to the rules; can be defended as valid.

Literate - someone who can read and write.

Lord, Lords - a man of high status, wealth and authority.

M

MP - a member of parliament.

Martyr - someone who willingly dies for or is killed due to their beliefs, usually religious.

Mass - an act of worship in the Catholic Church.

Medieval era, Medieval times, Middle Ages - the period from circa 1250 to 1500.

Mercenary - someone who takes action in order to earn money, rather than out of principle.

Middle class - refers to the socio-economic group which includes people who are educated and have professional jobs, such as teachers or lawyers.

Minister - a senior member of government, usually responsible for a particular area such as education or finance.

Miscarriage of justice - the conviction of a person for a crime they did not commit.

Monasteries, Monastery - a religious building occupied by monks.

Morals - a person's set of rules about what they consider right and wrong, used to guide their actions and behaviour.

Mutiny - a rebellion or revolt, in particular by soldiers or sailors against their commanding officers.

N

Nationalism, Nationalist, Nationalistic - identifying with your own nation and supporting its interests, often to the detriment or exclusion of other nations.

Navvy - a labourer involved in building railways, roads or canals.

Nobility - the social class ranked directly below royalty.

O

Oath - a solemn promise with special significance, often relating to future behaviour or actions.

Oath-helper - supporters of the accused in a medieval trial, or members of their local community who would support their oaths of innocence.

P

Parliament - a group of politicians who make the laws of their country, usually elected by the population.

Penal reform - a change to the law in an attempt to improve the system of legal punishment.

Persecute - to treat someone unfairly because of their race, religion or political beliefs.

Pillory - a device that trapped the neck and arms, used as a humiliating form of punishment. Located outdoors in a public place, criminals were locked into them for days at a time.

Pogrom - an organised attack on a certain group such as Jews in Eastern Europe.

Pope - the head of the Roman Catholic Church.

Population - the number of people who live in a specified place.

Poverty - the state of being extremely poor.

Preach, Preaching - to deliver a religious speech or sermon to a group of people.

Predecessor - the person who came before; the previous person to fill a role or position.

Prevent, Preventative, Preventive - steps taken to stop something from happening.

Printing press - a machine that reproduces writing and images by using ink on paper, making many identical copies.

Profit - generally refers to financial gain; the amount of money made after deducting buying, operating or production costs.

Prosecute - to institute or conduct legal proceedings against a person or organisation.

Puritan - a Protestant Christian who followed very strict moral rules.

R

Radical, Radicalism - people who want complete or extensive change, usually politically or socially.

Raid - a quick surprise attack on the enemy.

Rational - when something is based on reason or logic, like science.

Real wages - a person's income in terms of how much they can buy after taking inflation into account.

Rebellion - armed resistance against a government or leader, or resistance to other authority or control.

Rebels - people who rise in opposition or armed resistance against an established government or leader.

Recusancy - the refusal to attend Protestant church services.

Reform, Reforming - change, usually in order to improve an institution or practice.

Reign - a period of power, usually by a monarch.

Relief - something that reduces pressure on people, often through financial or practical support.

Repeal - to revoke or annul a law.

Repressive - a harsh or authoritarian action; usually used to describe governmental abuse of power.

Revolution - the forced overthrow of a government or social system by its own people.

Riots - violent disturbances involving a crowd of people.

Rookeries, Rookery - an area of densely populated housing, of poor quality and packed closely together.

S

Sanctity - the state of being holy or sacred; to have ultimate importance.

Sanitation - conditions relating to public health, such as the sewage system and drinking water supply.

Scandal, Scandalous - something that angers or shocks people because rules or accepted standards of behaviour have been broken.

Scapegoat - someone who is blamed for the wrongdoings or mistakes of others.

Separate system - a method of running prisons, tested at Pentonville, that involved keeping prisoners apart and alone for as much time as possible.

Sheriff, Sheriffs - an important royal official in medieval England, responsible for running the local court and ensuring tax was paid to the monarch.

Shire - a defined area of land in England during the Saxon and medieval periods, later known as a county.

Sin - in religion, an immoral act against God's laws.

Smog - thick fog caused by pollution, usually in cities.

Socialism - a political and economic system where most resources, such as factories and businesses, are owned by the state or workers with the aim of achieving greater equality between rich and poor.

Socialist - one who believes in the principles of socialism.

Standard of living - level of wealth and goods available to an individual or group.

State, States - an area of land or a territory ruled by one government.

Stocks - a restraining device that trapped the feet and ankles, used as a humiliating form of punishment. Located outdoors in a public place, criminals were locked into them for days at a time.

Strike - a refusal by employees to work as a form of protest, usually to bring about change in their working conditions. It puts pressure on their employer, who cannot run the business without workers.

Superior - better or higher in rank, status or quality.

Supernatural - an unscientific explanation for an event or manifestation unattributable to the laws of nature.

T

Tactic - a strategy or method of achieving a goal.

The crown, The throne - phrases used to represent royal power. For example, if someone 'seizes the throne' it means they have taken control. Can also refer to physical objects.

Treason - the crime of betraying one's country, often involving an attempt to overthrow the government or kill the monarch.

Tsar - the Russian word for emperor; can also be spelled 'czar'.

V

Vagabond, Vagrancy, Vagrant - someone who wanders from place to place and has neither home nor job.

W

Warrant - a document that allows something to happen legally, such as an arrest, search or administrative act.

Welfare - wellbeing; often refers to money and services given to the poorest people.

Wergild - meaning 'man price', this was the value placed on a man's life in Saxon England and the amount of compensation to be paid for his injury or death.

Workhouse - a place for poor people who were unable to work or support themselves.